TRIBE FINDING

Building Relationships as a
Path to Recovery

GERALD LOTT

S.H.E. PUBLISHING, LLC

TRIBE FINDING
Copyright © 2025 by Gerald Lott

For information contact:
Direct to Author: gerald.lott@svvor.org
Email: info@shepublishingllc.com
Website: www.shepublishingllc.com
MUNSTER, INDIANA | INDIANAPOLIS, INDIANA

Library of Congress Control Number: Forthcoming

ISBN:
978-1-964061-37-5 (paperback)
978-1-964061-38-2 (hardback)

First Edition: October 2025

10 9 8 7 6 5 4 3 2 1

Table of Contents

Prologue

I'm sitting in the waiting room of an auto dealership, where I spent 10 years of my life working various job titles. Luckily, I am not working here today. Today I am getting an oil change on a vehicle that I am literally wearing out on a daily basis, living my passion. I left my job here a little over five years ago to pursue a mission I believed was more important, to help people recover from their addictions to drugs and alcohol. When I walked away from my job at the dealership, I had no idea what the universe had in store for me. I have spent a considerable amount of my life trying to find my thing, my passion, my "why". I have also spent a good part of my life in recovery from a disease that I wouldn't wish on my worst enemy. If I had been told years ago that the two would be one and the same, I would not have believed it. I spent years trying to find validation, confidence and wealth in many avenues of life. I was a recording artist, a nightlife impresario, a restaurant owner, serial entrepreneur and too many jobs to mention. Though I could usually find a decent lifestyle, I never found "me". When I joined the world of recovery advocates and decided to dedicate my life to making it easier for people in my community to recover than to relapse, I finally found a life that I was happy to live.

I have been battling addiction in my life since high school. Things first came to a head in 1983 when I got kicked out of my high school with less than 3 months left in my senior year. (For the record, I will always claim that school as my alma mater for 2 reasons – 1) I did 3.75 years there and 2) My inner-alcoholic/addict has determined that this is the truth). After that, I went to college in New Orleans. The 4 year program took 5 years and some summers. I really enjoyed New Orleans. Where else does the whole city shut down all spring so I can drink and party? More on that later...

I am writing this book to discuss affinity grouping in recovery, a concept that I wish I could claim as my own invention. For those that are unfamiliar with the idea, we will be looking at the state of recovery from substance use disorders and co-occurring mental health issues with an emphasis on multiple pathways to recovery. This term, "multiple pathways" is a description of the various ways that people find recovery and the latest accepted definition of recovery as a whole. We'll be using the SAMHSA (Substance Abuse and Mental Health Services Administration) working definition of recovery as "a process of change through which individuals improve their health and wellness, live self-directed lives and strive to reach their full potential" as that is what most in the industry consider the current North Star. This definition begs distinction from the rigid abstinence based dogma of 100 years of 12 Step programs.

"Big Book Thumpers" (hard-core Alcoholics Anonymous devotees that live and breathe by the book) will tell you that there is only 1 recovery and that is to abstain from all mind and mood altering non-prescribed chemicals. Harm reduction advocates and many social workers will say recovery is the reduction in the chaotic lifestyles that can accompany drug and alcohol usage and one can be in recovery while using drugs and/or alcohol if it doesn't cause problems. Acknowledging multiple pathways to recovery allows for neither to be wrong. It also opens the door to new methodology, which for many years was either 'you join a "meeting"' or 'you "go it alone"'.

Today, people seeking recovery can find support in churches, support groups of all types and various activity clubs from yoga to rock climbing. For years, the general thought was to battle addiction with talking. Today, people are looking for opportunities to take their minds off their problems through action.

My goal in writing this volume is to explain how my team and I utilized affinity groups to help jumpstart the growth of our local recovery community. The sparks of the recovery fire in our small rural community were already burning when I arrived; I cannot take credit for that. I often joke that upon arriving here, I was informed they had "both kinds of recovery, AA and NA". Today, our community has many new options for people to meet and connect in positive, non-substance related ways. I credit my team of amazing Peer Support Workers and Administrators for pioneering that. These people have seen some of the worst that addiction can muster from people they are trying to help and they still meet every person that approaches with a welcoming smile. Our story is amazing, in that a miracle took place and a crackhead/alcoholic became a semi-responsible contributing member of society. I preface that statement with another; had it not been for the support and encouragement of my Sauk Valley Voices of Recovery (SVVOR) "Tribe", I would have returned to the dealership and asked for my job back. They are heroes and I stand in awe of every one of them.

Introduction to Tribes

Throughout this book, I will introduce you to some of the various tribes I have been a part of and some that I presently belong to. Some have been very positive influences on my life, some have been terrible, neutral or both good and bad. I am not great at maintaining social relationships. There are many more tribes I have exited than those I continue to participate in regularly. The same goes for people. I have known so many amazing and wonderful people in my life that I can't comprehend how I didn't value them more at the time. As people go through life intersecting with one another, it's astonishing how some of the most random and trivial conversations come back as through prophesy. I spent a short time as a manager on a small tour with a rock band out of Chicago called Pound Seven. For a few weeks, we travelled in a van across the country doing small gigs as a tribe. I don't know where those guys are today, but I recall a specific incident from a conversation about business we had as we drove past and noticed a company called Fast-Snap, has stuck with me and aided some of my life decisions for 25 years. This is the power of the tribe. As we tackle my story and how that relates to the concept of affinity grouping in recovery, I will introduce you to a few of the tribes I have experienced. My hope is to demonstrate how each tribe has contributed to my core structure and way of life, for better or worse

Lack of Connection is the Problem

I trace a lot of my addiction back to feeling like an outsider as a kid. In honor of the "it's hereditary" philosophy, I will admit that my maternal grandfather was an alcoholic and I was exposed to his "ism". I don't think that was what tripped my switch though.

I grew up in Chicago during the 1970s – early 80s. I was an only child of 2 comfortable, if not affluent Black professionals. While my father saw the city as his to roam, my mother spent her time almost exclusively on the South Side. We had a small bungalow home at the foot of Pill Hill, an upper middle class African-American neighborhood at the far south end of the city. I don't know why my parents made the academic decision they made for me; perhaps they thought they were providing the absolute best education available, or it was the ultimate status symbol. Whatever the reason, they sent me to an expensive, 99% white private school on the North Side. Today, with Uber and cell phones, that might not be a problem. Back then, it created a double whammy of isolation for me.

I lived in a black neighborhood on the far South Side, but every morning, I woke up early (too early) to catch a ride to the other side of town with another child's family. We were in the car for about an hour and a half facing traffic every morning. We got to school just as the bell rang and ran into class. To say we were well educated is an understatement. I learned to see the world from the same place that the children of the 1% did. I understood their values and even grew to share them. I became a pretty good soccer player, and was halfway decent with a tennis racquet and hockey stick. I sucked at basketball. I rallied on standardized tests that were slanted toward the Anglo life experience. If I had been a young white kid, I would be doing pretty well. The problem was the fact that I was a black kid from the South side. The minute the school day ended, I had to make a beeline for the bus stop. An hour and a half in a car was easily 2.5 hours on the bus. School let out at 2:30pm. I usually made it home by 5pm. By then, everyone in my neighborhood was inside for the night.

This was my life. All week long, I "missed" everything. I got to school after the "happened before school" excitement and left before the "kids stayed at school and…" conversations. Then I got home after all the kids on the block went in for the night. I didn't know the neighborhood kids my classmates spoke of, and I didn't know the classmates my neighborhood friends had. I was the perpetual outsider.

On top of my geographic estrangement, I was culturally separated. This was before social media and the internet made the world small. In those days, there were real differences in the clothes, music and lifestyles of people from different sides of the city. I remember getting Sporto duck boots because they were cool at school. I was ridiculed mercilessly at home for them or trying to explain the intricacies of the band Kiss to fans of the Brothers Johnson.

My awkwardness must have been noticeable. When I finished 8th grade, my mother decided to send me to a school where I would be around more black kids. I still went to school outside the neighborhood, but it was closer and more kids from my neighborhood went there. It was a strict Jesuit high school. Mom probably thought I needed some religion too. Unfortunately, I was still the outsider. I had never really learned how to fit in. I sat at the lunch table of the kids that I thought I was supposed to associate with. These were the other Black kids that transferred in from the private schools around the city. Most of these kids had been together since pre-school at the University of Chicago Lab School. Most of our parents were friends or acquaintances. We represented few neighborhoods and cliques. We laughed and hung out, but I never fully attached. I was always a spectator of sorts and always felt alone.

I have heard many people around the tables of AA talk about how they walked into their first meeting and—BLAMMO!—they knew in their soul that they'd found their people. That wasn't my story. As an arrogant, entitled, and fearful young Black man, I found every reason in the world to set myself apart. I was too smart, too young, too rich, or too poor. I was a "me," and they were "them"; never would there be common ground.

For over 20 years, I was in and out of the doors of AA. I was smart enough to pick up on what they were saying and say it back with sufficient authority to make someone believe I understood it. I almost did, but anyone that is in a 12 step program will tell you – You can understand it and still not live it. I was a pretender. I sat through meetings and spoke a pretty good game, but I was completely miserable until the next relapse.

I started off at the Lincoln Park Alano Club in Chicago. The treatment center would take us each Sunday morning to a Gratitude Meeting there. It was the easiest meeting in the world! When it was your turn, you simply said your name and something you were grateful for. As simple as, "I'm Gerald, an alcoholic and today I am grateful to be here with all of you." I hope you can see the overt conman in that statement. Anyway,

I thought that was "The Program". As long as I was grateful, I wouldn't drink... it wasn't and I did.

I would bounce around to a lot of meetings within those 20 years. Sometimes even finding my way back to the Lincoln Park AA Club. I never gave in though. I never said I was part of any group and I belonged there. There were just too many differences and our similarities weren't enough. Yes, I considered myself an alcoholic, but I was also a drug addict. I wasn't supposed to talk about that. For those unaware, many "old-timers" in AA really hold true to the AA tradition that seeks to keep AA solely about alcohol. Even though most people these days are using multiple substances, there are AA tables where one does not mention their drug use. This can be good and bad – good, the conversation stays within a predictable zone – bad, some people continue to use drugs because it is a "separate" issue. For me, alcohol and drugs are of the same source and outcome.

There was an AA meeting in 1990 or 91 at a Park Fieldhouse in Chicago on Addison Ave, about 3 miles west of Wrigley Field. I went there on Friday nights, determined to build myself into the "gang". It was a solid meeting with 30-40 people, mostly white, probably blue-collar and it seemed to skew 40-60 years old. Week after week, I went. I was the only black person there, 25 years old and had just failed out of law school. During the meetings, I was all good. I could talk program and Big Book. I even knew when to throw in a little mention of God to get the crowd on my side. Eventually, I invited myself along with a large group of people that went to the Denny's or IHOP or whatever little restaurant was about a block away. I never felt more lonely, different or out of place than sitting at that table. I had no idea who these people were or what their lives were about. I had never ridden a Harley or listened to Lynyrd Skynyrd. The stories they told about people from the old neighborhood meetings went right past me; I had no idea who "Old Tom H" was, nor did I give a fuck. Likewise, no one ever really seemed terribly interested in me. It was like nobody was going to say I couldn't come but... I tried that for a few weeks then stopped going to the restaurant and the meeting. There was nothing there for me. Point to note, this could have all been my own crazy. Maybe they were welcoming and I missed it. The fact is, it doesn't matter. I am in no way saying they did anything wrong. It just wasn't for me and sometimes, that is neutral. Neither good nor bad.

So how could it be that I was OK at the 6pm meeting, but a bust at the 7pm social? Simple, I had the common denominator at the meeting. That was about being an alcoholic and I had that covered. The meeting after the meeting was something different. That was "Tribe". That was people that knew one another and had "else" in common. The "else" being the history of commonalities. That was something I wasn't to be a part of any more than those people would fit in at a Naughty by Nature concert. (How about that 90's reference?) The simple reality is, my disease can hold me in a group that is solely focused on the disease of it. But in life, I, as with everyone else, try to suffocate my disease. I try to push it out. IF the only thing I have in common with someone is that disease, then I am essentially doing the same to them.

I call to the conversation the University of Sussex experiment of the stinky shirt. A sociologist named Reicher theorized that people generally have a gut level aversion to others and that the key to group cohesion is the ability to minimize the disgust people have for one another. I know this disgust all too well. I cannot call myself a germaphobe, but I certainly don't want to touch or come into anything other than incidental contact with people I don't know. That shifts significantly upon me learning a person's name and having even the slightest conversation. This is exactly what the Sweaty Shirt Experiment held true. In it, a group of college students at Sussex University were made to sniff sweaty t-shirts from people they had never met. They were told the wearers of the shirts were other students, either from Sussex or from the rival, Brighton University down the road. After sniffing the shirts, the students ranked their level of disgust. The outcome was considerable in that students indicated lower levels of repulsion when they thought the shirt was of a Sussex student. "It shows us how important our ways are in which we define group boundaries. It has implications for issues of social exclusion, prejudice and discrimination. It's about how we define ourselves, who is 'us' and who is 'other'," said Reicher.

I didn't realize it when it was happening, but winter cold and the COVID-19 pandemic were a great experiment in tribe finding. To be more direct, it was actually the opposite of tribe finding. Many people have reported that their recovery was challenged when they had to distance themselves from their in-person support systems and fellowships. Just a few years after this great experiment, we see all sorts of sociological impact from the isolation.

> Since the onset of the COVID-19 pandemic, there have been various impacts on societal well-being; not only have many people had to face the potentiality of COVID-19 infection and death, but they have also had to struggle through economic collapse and social isolation due to quarantine measures. In correlation with these problems, there has been a significant increase in those who report symptoms of mental illness. Compared to 1 in 10 adults in 2019, 4 in 10 American adults have reported symptoms of anxiety or depression throughout the course of the pandemic 1. Given that up to 50% of those with substance use disorders (SUDs) experience symptoms of mental illness, reports of substance abuse have been on the rise as well. Substance use disorder, also known as drug addiction, occurs when a physiological or psychological dependence on a drug develops that leads to an inability to control one's use. According to the Centers

> for Disease Control and Prevention (CDC), 13% of Americans have reported increasing or starting substance use as a way of coping with stress related to the pandemic 2. An overdose reporting system known as ODMAP also reported an 18% increase nationwide in opiate overdoses

3. As noted by behavioral psychologist William Stoops, "There's sort of a perfect storm of factors that we know increase drug use. People are stressed and isolated, so they make unhealthy decisions, including drinking and taking drugs".

Chacon NC, Walia N, Allen A, Sciancalepore A, Tiong J, Quick R, Mada S, Diaz MA, Rodriguez I. Substance use during COVID-19 pandemic: impact on the underserved communities. Discoveries (Craiova). 2021 Dec 31;9(4):e141. doi: 10.15190/d.2021.20. PMID: 35261922; PMCID: PMC8896880.

The detrimental impact of social isolation emerged as a cross-cutting theme (Table 2). Providers expressed that prior to the COVID-19 pandemic, their clients depended on social connection, in-person services and groups, as well as access to resources to maintain recovery for their SUD or mental health condition. Social isolation was, "the worst thing for anybody with mental health or substance abuse" conditions. One provider noted that social isolation was a risk factor for their clients, "because the opposite of addiction is connection." Providers reported that some clients chose to risk COVID-19 exposure rather than staying isolated.

That's probably the most prominent, the isolation. Some people would rather risk exposure than be isolated. That's been pretty common across the board among most of the people I've talked to. One of the biggest issues they're experiencing is the isolation, lack of community and connection.

Social isolation had a largely negative, pervasive impact on the overall wellbeing of their clients and was a catalyst for negative outcomes, including return to substance use, increased substance use, fatal and non-fatal overdose and an exacerbation of mental health symptoms.

Providers reported feeling the impact of recovery support groups such as Alcoholics Anonymous (AA) or Narcotics Anonymous (NA), which reduced as they moved online. Furthermore, they reported that many of their clients did not like the virtual format. Providers also reported the importance of facilitating in-person groups because they could better assess how their clients were doing, and felt their clients enjoyed connecting with others who were also in treatment and were positively influenced by others also in recovery.

Providers reported that social isolation fueled chaotic, increased use of substances among clients. The pandemic magnified many of the issues that clients were reportedly experiencing, including mental illness, SUD and homelessness.

Jeffers A, Meehan AA, Barker J, Asher A, Montgomery MP, Bautista G, Ray CM, Laws RL, Fields VL, Radhakrishnan L, Cha S, Christensen A, Dupervil B, Verlenden JV, Cassell CH, Boyer A,

DiPietro B, Cary M, Yang M, Mosites E, Marcus R. Impact of Social Isolation during the COVID-19 Pandemic on Mental Health, Substance Use, and Homelessness: Qualitative Interviews with Behavioral Health Providers. Int J Environ Res Public Health. 2022 Sep 25;19(19):12120. doi: 10.3390/ijerph191912120. PMID: 36231422; PMCID: PMC9566547.

My Story of Recovery

I returned from College in New Orleans with a huge drug problem. I will get into some of that later, but my recovery journey starts in earnest in 1988 when I first went to in-patient treatment. I was lucky - I was still on my parents' insurance, so I could go pretty much anywhere. I found a bed at a treatment center in Lincoln Park in Chicago. For those unaware, Lincoln Park is one of the nicer areas in Chicago. It lies just off the Lake Michigan Beaches to the north of the Downtown area. In just about every movie about Chicago, you'll see an overhead shot of the skyline with the John Hancock Building and the Drake Hotel. Those shots are from Lincoln Park. Though I grew up on the far south side of the city, I attended grade school in Lincoln Park (across the street from the Zoo) so I knew the area and was very comfortable there. If I had to go to a treatment center, this was the right one.

I don't remember the specific name of the program, that hospital has long been torn down and turned into multi-million dollar townhomes. I think it was just called Lincoln Park Hospital. Whatever the name was, their program was a straightforward 28 day reprogramming aimed at total abstinence from all mind and mood-altering substances including alcohol. I can remember the intake interview when the counselor was questioning me and I adamantly insisted I didn't want to give up all alcohol for the rest of my life, because I wanted to be able to have a glass of fine wine sometime in the future. And anyway, my real problem was cocaine. I guess I was picturing myself sitting in Paris at an outdoor bistro on a spring evening with a beret, a loaf of bread and a bottle of their best vino being quite sophisticated. "Have you ever had a glass of fine wine?" The Counselor asked. I shook my head, "No". And that was that, my fantasy was squashed. I then went on to say I wanted to quit cigarettes. To that, the Counselor said, "Let's deal with what's killing you in the immediate." I would go on to smoke Marlboro Reds for another 30 years. I really wish we'd just lumped it all together.

That treatment center was the first one. As I said, insurance paid for it, parents visited and sent cakes, moreover, every morning the staff took us for long walks through Lincoln Park Zoo. I loved those early sunrise walks as the group strolled past the big cat enclosures and such. The sun was rising over the lake and the animals stretched and yawned. The world was peaceful and I was taken care of. Maybe I liked treatment too much... I went back to treatment so many times that I lost count and can't remember all the different places. I literally recall driving by a building that looks familiar and suddenly remember eating jello in the dayroom there.

I don't remember much of that first treatment, but I was on the 8th floor. There were men and women. It was fairly nice and the food was probably pretty good. There is a quote attributed to Maya Angelou where she says *"I've learned that people will forget what you said, people will forget what you did, but people will never forget how you made them feel."* That sums up my stay at Lincoln Park Hospital's Drug Treatment Program. There was not a thing that was said to me that I remember with regard to how to stay off drugs. I remember my feelings. I recall feeling like a failure and a disappointment because of the look in my parents' eyes when they visited. My father just couldn't wrap his head around this and my mother was pissed off. I remember feeling at home and comfortable because I had no responsibility, plenty of people to talk to and a fairly defined schedule. It felt like day-camp for fucked-up grownups. I also felt superior. After a few days of the revolving door, I wasn't the new guy anymore. I became the "Welcome" Guy. "Here, let me show you all around". I also felt fear. There was a man that was assigned to my room toward the end of my stay at LPH; I don't recall his name. He was a huge African-American man and I seem to recall he worked in construction. I felt a kinship with him because we were the only black people in the hospital at that time. I just remember that he seemed bigger, stronger and tougher than me. He was a heroin user and was going through withdrawals directly in front of me. For days, he lay there writhing in pain and vomiting. It was the scariest thing I had ever seen. I didn't know heroin. To the world, I was a crack smoker, but I was stuck up, so I considered myself to be addicted to "free-basing". You know, like Richard Pryor... The funny thing is, today, I preach that you can't scare someone out of using drugs. But that week in LPH, watching a man withdrawing from heroin, scared me. I went on to have a long career of drug use and NEVER tried heroin or a needle and I know it is because of what I witnessed in that treatment center.

My father hit me with a gem sometime around this first treatment. He pulled me to the side and said, "You know, everybody is making money off this, but you. The guys that sold it to you made money and the people getting you off it are getting paid. Where's your money?" That sat with me. It still does... He put it in a way that made me look through my own eyes and I did not like what I saw, but I couldn't stop. It wasn't for lack of trying and at great expense to my family. I would go into treatment and come out to have various lengths of sobriety. Many times it was short, a month or so. Sometimes I would make it a year without a drink or drug. The single biggest truth is, I never changed. Treatment can stop someone from using if they are willing to stay there and play by the rules. For 28 days, you are occupied in a fairly stress-less and controlled environment with little access to your drug of choice. You can stop, but recovery demands that I stay "stopped". A friend of mine named Terry P. in Rockford, IL says, "Meetings and treatment are the pit stop, the race is out there in the streets". Facts are facts, I have to stay sober when I am not being watched all day, fed and given 24 hour counseling. That's where the rubber meets the road.

My last "treatment" was and wasn't treatment. It was a jail with treatment in it. I spent 4 months in Division 8 of Cook County Jail in 1994. In a series of events that I can only attribute to God's hand, I landed in Gateway Foundation's program in the jail and it changed me and my life forever. I wish I could say I never had another drink or drug after it, but I have. I will just tell you that I finally found one of the ends of the path and it shook me.

Here's how I got there. My mother passed away soon after the birth of my first child, Jordan. Due to several factors that I will discuss later, I was actively using when she died and I didn't handle things well, at all. Being an only child with no one to turn to for support, I moved into her house after she died. Several family members and friends had come into my mother's home after her death and pilfered her furs and jewelry while telling me I wasn't welcome due to my state of intoxication. When I finally gained access to the house, I found that there wasn't much left. I began doing what I know, I took anything of value I could find and began trading it for crack. I was using so much that a dealer came to the house with me and gave me a bunch on credit. Eventually, he said that I needed to pay up or sign the house over to him. I explained that I couldn't do that because I didn't know if it was legally in my name. At that point, he told me that he'd kill me if I couldn't find a way to pay him. I panicked. I told him that I could get him a gun. I had been going to my father's house during the day to use and swipe change and I knew where he kept his handgun. My plan was to trade it. The dealer drove me to my father's house and I tried to use my key. The lock wouldn't turn. He had changed the lock. I tried to crawl through a window and tripped the burglar alarm. I ran to the keypad to enter the code and to my surprise... that too had been changed. Within minutes, I was watching the police pull up to the house. I had been arrested a few months earlier for a crime I absolutely did not commit and I was out on bail pending trial. This new arrest meant I would not be eligible for another release. I was headed to Cook County Jail and I was going to be there a while.

I can only believe my father pulled some serious strings during my incarceration. I went into the jail and within a few days, I was transferred to the Gateway Drug Program in Division 8. Compared to the other tiers, Division 8 was a cakewalk. Nevertheless, it was still Cook County Jail, one of the toughest county jails in the country. I was scared to death. This was a world I was ill-prepared for. I find it interesting that within a relatively short period of time, I lost the fear and accepted the situation as my deserved fate. Compared to some of the other treatment centers I have been to, the jail was ghastly, but I somehow came to be comfortable and even enjoy my time there. I saw some terrible things in that jail and I learned that there is always someone tougher, meaner or crazier than me. I also learned that I never want to go back.

That wasn't my only significant brush with the law. For a time, it seemed that I couldn't go more than a week without some interaction with the police. I wear my hair very low and cut it myself. As I do so, I run my hand along a slight indentation of my skull. It's barely noticeable among the many imperfections that I am, but it is a reminder of the wreckage of my past. It comes from the boot of a Chicago police officer. I won't do him the service to know or care about his name.

On this particular day, I think I was running towards jail from the moment I woke up. There were times when my body and mind just knew I needed a break. On this day, I recall walking past a small corner restaurant in Wicker Park, where I had eaten a 100 times. It was a nicer little breakfast place that was popular with the 20 and 30 something crowd. On Saturday mornings, people would stand on the sidewalk waiting for a table while moms pushed strollers between them heading for the park. I clearly remember walking through the crowd, hoping I didn't recognize anyone and being keenly aware that I had to pay my daily fare for my addiction.

I needed money in the worst way possible. So, though my shame kept my head down, my eyes were up scanning for opportunity. I wasn't a good burglar. I wasn't the guy in the movie that studied and made a plan. I was more of an alley cat stalking around looking for any hole in a wall or fence to slide through. It never left my mind that less than a year ago, I drove these streets in expensive cars and fine clothes. Here I was again, looking for an open gate, a garage door that was left open, a set of tools inadvertently left on a porch.

I was a few doors past the restaurant when I came upon what seemed like a hit. I found an open wrought iron gate with a beautiful brick house behind it. I stepped through the gate as though walking to the front door and when I thought I was clear, I slid to the side of the house and began looking for a way in. I had no idea what I might've found in that home. I didn't know if there were riches beyond my dreams or if the score would simply be a half gallon of milk and a stapler. Whatever I could find, I would take... I got to the rear of the house and I couldn't see a way in.

I did, however, see the garage door was open slightly, so I went in. In the garage, I found the usual stuff, a few hand tools, car supplies, a bike with a flat tire. I also found a bag on a counter. It looked like the owner might have taken the bag out of the car when they returned home and accidentally left it while carrying in a child or groceries. I opened the bag and to my surprise, I found something. It was a 35mm camera with 3 or 4 lens attachments. That's what I needed. Mission accomplished! I zipped up the bag and headed out of the garage. As I poked out into the sunlight, I heard a voice say something to the effect of "Hey You! Stop! Police!" The people standing in front of the restaurant didn't recognize me as one of their own, but instead a dope fiend going into the yard of a million dollar home. They had called the police while I was lurking on the side of the house. I dropped the camera bag, slammed through the back gate into the alley and put my years of soccer training to use. I ran down the alley towards the street with a cop about 30 feet behind me. Years of being chased by good guys and bad guys had taught me some tricks. Try not to cross streets - Don't run in straight lines too long - get to the middle of the street so people don't jump out from the side. I rounded the first corner and could feel the officer fall back a bit. I hit the second corner wide and moved over to the middle of the street. That's when I put the burners on. Looking back, I could see that I had the cop beat. He was a good 200 feet behind me and losing ground. Problem - my zigs and zags had me now running directly back towards the restaurant where 3 police cars were waiting. I can remember a voice from the sidewalk saying, "Here he is now!" and suddenly 3 or 4 more police joined the chase. I ran past the restaurant and somehow they didn't grab me. I made it 2 or 3 more blocks before my stamina just turned off. I had to stop. I made a quick corner and found a basement doorway to duck into.

In a minute or so, 2 cops found me and with guns drawn on me while out of breath, I lay down, spread-eagle on my stomach. By the time the first 2 had cuffs on me, the first responding officer that had run me out of the garage finally caught up. He said, "You're a fast fucker," then he kicked me in the head with his boot. I blacked out and my memory jumped to being in the police station. I was never treated for a head injury though and I have had pain in that spot for years. Today, it is just a small indent I can feel when I rub my hand over my head. It is a reminder of where my addiction took me and who I had become. It also reminds me that I was lucky. Once you get into that type of situation with the police, anything can happen. What if that officer, "Mr. Kick a Guy on the ground" had decided to shoot me while I was running? The remnant of that incident always reminds me of how lucky I am to be alive. That my God must have a purpose for me.

I recently saw a gentleman speak on recovery that had written a book some time ago. He talked about how he was still using when he wrote the book and said that is why it's so "raw". When it was Q & A time, I asked what he would say differently if he wrote the book now with 9 years of sobriety. He replied that it would be more about all the benefits of living in recovery - greater family times, self-esteem and positive things like that. That is where I am today. As I write this, I have just celebrated 17 years of continuous sobriety. I remember the crazy times, but not as clearly as I recall the last decade and a half of recovery. Today, my story doesn't start with statements like "You won't believe how nuts this was..." My stories today all seem to find a way to include the statement "and that's when God stepped in and made things better."

In 1993, I was blessed by a friend of mine to try a geographic cure. My friend was living in Atlanta and working as a really successful music producer there. Knowing I was struggling in Chicago, he invited me to stay at his place in Atlanta for a while. Great for me, terrible for him. I took advantage of the situation, ran the streets and generally did everything I could to live as close to the edge without tipping over it. I began running around with some music industry people and wanna-be's. I was clean and sober at the time, but it was an expensive lifestyle. My girlfriend was pregnant back in Chicago and I was on a mission to find some way to make millions quickly. I was spending money quick, fast and foolishly. At the time, my main source of income was residual payments from a couple radio/tv commercials I had been in. The checks would arrive at my mother's house and she would forward them to me. Well, Mom noticed how rapidly I was spending money and she had seen this pattern before. She assumed I was "back using the stuff". I wasn't, but I couldn't convince her since I had lied about it so many times before. She simply stopped sending the checks to me. She said they must be getting lost in the mail. As you can guess, I went from concerned to worried, to stressed, to "out of my mind". As weeks passed with no money and her saying the post office people couldn't tell her anything new, my overzealous pursuit of this money only served to confirm her suspicions. However, I wasn't using... I was running out of time to get out of Arnold's place. I was running up big tabs with people that were willing to front me a few bucks. I was walking, because I didn't have money to buy gas, and to make things worse, I wasn't willing to get a job. So I went home to Chicago. That last week in Atlanta, I let my inner-addict out and it was bad. I returned to Chicago with a severe case of disappointment and resentment. I actually saw myself as a victim. Funny thing is, during my entire time in Atlanta, the thought of getting a real job never crossed my mind.

Shortly after I returned, I found myself at my mother's house. For some reason, she sent me to the trunk of her car to get something. When I opened the trunk, I saw a green Marshall Field's department store bag. Those bags had always contained goodies since I was a child. New clothes, new toys... sometimes it was their delicious Frango Mint Meltaways! I opened the bag and there were goodies for sure. I found dozens of residual checks - the checks I had been waiting for, amounting to 10's of thousands of dollars. I flew into a rage. I stormed back into the house and confronted my mother! "You lying B____! You said these never came. You ruined my life. I could have been something!" The only other overly dramatic thing I could have said was, "I could've been a contender..." I showed her. I had the checks now. I ran back out, stole her car and went on a 2-week bender with the checks. I didn't return until every single penny was gone.

My mother passed away while I was on that run. I returned home to a call from my dad asking if I could handle bad news. She had cancer and it took her quickly. She found out she had a tumor in her sinus cavity one week and died when it metastasized the next week. I now live with the fact that we argued the last time I saw her and I said some terrible things to her, things I didn't mean and things meant to hurt her. I carry deep shame and regret over that scene from my life. So much that I couldn't bring myself to attend her funeral. Today, I believe she is part of God's universal wisdom and knows that my feelings were not what I demonstrated in that moment. That is my hope.

I stayed relatively sober (no drugs or alcohol, but oh my God, I was crazy) from the time my mother passed in 1994 until 2008. For that 14 years, I pursued life feeling abandoned and put myself in horribly awkward and non-productive situations. I managed and promoted nightclubs and lived in the music business full-tilt. I was the guy in our crew to hold the drugs, thinking no one would suspect me. My friends and associates were pretty major drug dealers and the ones that weren't, tried to look like they were. We wanted flash and street cred. I went to nightclubs pretty much every single night and spent the early evenings in strip clubs, spending money I couldn't afford on women that didn't have any interest in me. I was sober, if you consider I had no chemicals in my bloodstream.

In 2008, my world seemed to crash and I relapsed. Luckily it was pretty short lived. In the course of about 4-6 months of using, I was able to get rid of everything and everybody in my life. I popped out on the other side broken, beat and looking for a new way.

I had tried every option I could to stay in my world and get sober. This time, when I asked for help, the universe did me a tremendous favor. I called the office of the sober living homes that I had lived in 15 years earlier and (God Moment!) a guy that I had known back then answered. He said he remembered me and when I asked to come home, he said I was welcomed. They didn't have a bed in Chicago, but he said he would give me a month free if I was willing to go to Rockford (1.5 hours away). I jumped at it and the rest is the subject of this book. If I had not been introduced to the Rockford recovery scene and engaged with it, I would be dead, because I wasn't going to make it much further when I called.

On April 17, 2008, I moved to the sober living home in Rockford. I will discuss the recovery in community in that town a little later, but suffice it to say, I found sobriety there. I would go on to live and work in Rockford for 3 years. I recall that after a while my children would come visit me. One day in 2009, I decided to tell my 11-year-old son how I had big plans to come back to Chicago and make everything right again. I'd re-open the restaurant, get a fancy house, and plant gumdrop trees in the backyard. It was some real rainbows and unicorn stuff. They say you get the best truths from the mouths of children, and this was no exception. My son looked in my face and said, "You know Dad, when you're in Chicago you're really weird and crazy. You seem much nicer here, and I like being around you." He continued, "It's a long way to come see you and we don't see you as much, but I like seeing you here more than back in Chicago."

First, I picked my face up off the floor. This child could see what I couldn't. Chicago was no longer a place where I could survive, let alone thrive. It was at that moment that I knew I had to stay out of Chicago for good. I lived in Rockford for a few years and started building a new life. I eventually met a woman, and we began dating. As life goes, we got pregnant and decided to move to her hometown a little outside of Rockford.

Life in Rural Dixon

I moved to the small town of Dixon, IL because that is where my partner grew up and had family. Our family was growing and we needed to be around grandparents and extended family to help with watching the children. For about a year, I continued to work at an auto dealership about an hour away in Rockford. It was a huge dealership chain that had stores all over the region. I had connected with them because they had a store in Dixon but would let me start off at the Rockford location. Though my address was in Dixon, my life was elsewhere. I left town as the sun rose every day and returned after nightfall. Eventually, the time came for me to transfer to the company's dealership in Dixon. The saving of 2+ hours each day in commute allowed me to be more involved with my family, save on fuel and begin to explore my community.

Dixon is a small rural town about 100 miles west of Chicago. Nestled in the cornfields, this small town of 18,000 people is famous for being home to a prison and the childhood home of President Ronald Reagan. More recently, the City Comptroller embezzled $50 million to raise champion show horses. Most of the people here know each other, and have since childhood. This is the kind of place where people mark time and geography by who lived where. Example – they used to play baseball on the field next to where Tom Jaskin had the house that was always under construction. I recently had a conversation with the City Manager at a social event and we started talking about the character of the community. He remarked that people are "super-nice but a little guarded". To me, they are the type of people that wave to you across the street. "Across the street" being the operative word. So why this dissection of Dixon? Because here I came, an outsider. My wife isn't much of a social butterfly. She prefers home and her small circle of friends. I met a few people at work, but none that clicked with me in the way that formed long lasting relationships. I don't claim racism, but I am aware that being black in this small, mostly white, rural, mid-western town didn't really open any doors either. I was just on the fringes of the community. I remember going to the cleaners to pick up my clothes and the cleaner knew me by name. I thought I was amazing and memorable. My wife reminded me, "You're like one of 3 black people in town that wear a suit and tie to work..." I eventually found my people though on the basketball court at the local YMCA.

Another benefit of the transfer was the morning freedom. Instead of leaving at 6:30am to drive across the state, I could play pick-up basketball at the YMCA on Mondays, Wednesdays and Fridays at 6am with a regular group of guys around my age. Having no other exercise or outlet for aggression, I played religiously for years. The guys I met at the Y became my first local friends and acquaintances. These were the guys I bumped into at the store and stood to talk with about politics. I bought insurance from a guy that played and the Police Chief played as well. I sold cars to these guys and learned which local restaurants were good from them. They recommended a realtor, handyman or electrician.

The slow pace of Dixon worked for me. I was so used to the hustle of Chicago plus I had constant anxiety due to my history and imagined need to compete with the people I grew up around. In Chicago, I always felt like I was being judged and I was never up to par. I needed material things, cool associations and astounding feats to measure up. In Dixon, I felt somewhat anonymous. For some reason, I didn't feel the same need to impress anyone. I drove a few years old Ford Explorer and wore clothes I bought at Kohl's. I was an "everyman" blending into the scenery. However, every time I had to go to Chicago, my mindset would shift as I got closer. As I stated, we are about 100 miles due west of the city along 1 highway. As I merged on to the highway, I was content with my life and all was good. The closer I got to Chicago, the more I wanted. I needed my Explorer to morph into a Porsche. I often would stop at Nordstorm's on the way to pick up some outfit replacement - a shirt, tie, shoes -

something expensive to make me feel competitive. I hate to recall this thinking, because I was stone cold sober and still had these chaotic behaviors.

Dixon was good for me, but there was no real recovery community like I had seen in Rockford. There were AA meetings but I wasn't terribly drawn to their style of 12 step. I had most recently found sobriety in a hotbed of recovery around very disciplined long-term AA members. In Rockford, I surrounded myself with people that truly tried to hold fast to the pages of the Big Book of Alcoholics Anonymous. We are not saints. Many of us struggled, but we tried. What I found in Dixon meetings was much looser. There were people that rambled on about unrelated topics, old-timers that actively said they didn't believe in the steps, arguments and crosstalk in the meeting hall and plenty of "13th Stepping", that's what they call it when you use the program to create sexual relationships with newcomers.

I hear that style of 12 step worked for some. It wasn't working for me. I found myself taking every day that I had off and driving an hour back to Rockford to attend meetings and hang out with my sober friends. You can imagine the toll that took on family time. I talked to a few people that I knew in Dixon that shared some of my opinions and we decided to start our own meeting. Of course, it took a while to get going. There was resistance from some at the old meeting, who sarcastically called our meeting the "Structure Meeting" because they resented us asking people to stay on topic and be considerate by not going on 10 minute monologues when others in the room hadn't had a chance to speak. We persisted. That meeting is now 9 or 10 years old and has a strong following, but it took time. A good portion of my philosophy of connection and community comes from this experience. Had I not created that meeting and its subsequent network of likeminded attendees, I would have lost my family due to my absence or lost my program, because I didn't have time to travel. Both options lead to the same place in my mind - I drink and drug.

When I took on my RCO (Recovery Community Organization) job, I committed to work to make recovery more accessible to more people in my community. Being very familiar with the recovery scene, I knew there were many strata within the community. I had seen the old timers at AA tell someone they should find another meeting because they identified themselves as an "addict". I have seen All Recovery Groups where you can discuss any problem at all, from alcoholism to gambling to porn addiction. Religious groups, yoga, acupuncture and intellectual "out-thinking my addiction" concepts, all had found traction in the global space. So why was it that the only options in my small town were AA and NA? What would be the solution if I find those groups aren't working for me or I don't feel comfortable with someone that attends a particular group? There had to be another way.

As I started working with hardcore addicts and alcoholics, I would spend a great deal of time driving them to detox or treatment centers. In our conversations, I would talk to them about their previous attempts to get sober. I always asked if they had ever tried a 12-step program. I can't count how many times I heard them reply "Yeah, it just wasn't for me..." Let's translate – "I went, I didn't understand it. I didn't feel different immediately and the people there weren't my usual crew. They looked clean and happy and open and I didn't feel any of those things. So I stopped going..." That is the most important part of the statement. "So I stopped going..." Everything else can come in time, but when the person stops going, it's over. So my goal became finding the solution to that problem. How do I keep people coming?

I love my groups. From my immediate family group to my AA Home Group (New Solutions in Dixon, IL – We meet every Wednesday morning at 9am at the Church of the Brethren). From my office work group to the guys I have been playing basketball with 3 mornings a week for the better part of the last decade. I saw those groups threatened during the Covid-19 pandemic. As gathering became more and more difficult, groups changed, some disappeared altogether. It's not lost on me which reappeared. My family never left or broke apart. We needed one another and had no other options. My Home Group took some time off, but as we realized that zoom meetings weren't providing the same connections, we resumed in person. Basketball took a little longer to reconvene, but it did. However I must admit that our numbers suffered. What never changed was the "whys" of my grouping. Why do I need my immediate family and why do they need me? Why do I need my support group? Why do I need my athletic partners? Each has a unique reason, but a reason nonetheless.

When my RCO was first getting started, we were blessed with a grant to hire people that were very new in recovery. I was fortunate to find two young men that wanted to help launch our programs. Both happened to be members of the LGBTQ+ community. While both were out and proud, they were dealing with issues resulting from their identity. As things ramped up with our RCO and our lives became a little more stressful, both relapsed into their SUD. The interesting thing is that one attached himself to a gay friend of our program that is solidly in recovery and working as a Recovery Coach. My employee asked this friend to sponsor him. They launched Crystal Meth Anonymous in our area. They connected with a strong LGBTQ+ recovery community in Chicago and attended various events, retreats, and conferences. He found his tribe and started thriving. He is now about 7 months sober and has accepted a job as a Recovery Support Specialist with another organization. I am extremely proud of him.

My other employee has not enjoyed the same success. His path has taken him further towards his bottom. He had never accepted the idea of support meetings, so he was basically running on will power and stubbornness. He got into a relationship and went from 0 to 100 in no time flat. The relationship was volatile, and the boyfriend was extremely controlling – or so we were told. He often chose to leave work and social events early or miss them altogether to be with his partner. As I am sure you can predict, the employee started having little "slips" then bigger ones until he found himself in a full-on binge. The relationship ended and that sent him further into a tailspin using meth. I am very sad to say that as of just a short time prior to this writing, he was still struggling and finding it hard to ask for help.

My Thief Tribe

My life has been an interesting series of community building followed by drug-fueled bridge burning. I have a great friend named Todd that I have known since I was a small child. We went to rival grade schools, attended the same high school and then were college roommates. Todd can tell you today where just about everyone he's met in his life is living and what they are doing. I, on the other hand, have lost contact with so many people, that I often forget we ever knew each other at all. I know this seems like a bit of a ramble but I promise, it's going somewhere.

Each of my drug runs has had its own community. These days, the opioid crisis has led harm reduction advocates to suggest people not to use drugs alone. They say this as a safety protocol because people that lose consciousness due to overdose have a better chance if someone is there to help them. I have found that I cannot do drugs alone, not because I fear overdose but because I need the word-of-mouth network to even find my supply. I need people to help me find drugs, run the scams I need to feed the habit and honestly, to do the drugs with me.

In college I was part of the "weed head" crew. We spent most of our days seeking or smoking weed. I returned to Chicago after graduating and immediately connected with my high school party crew. They were still selling and using massive amounts of drugs. When I told them I was heading to law school, we hatched a plan that I would become the gang's lawyer someday. I took an ounce of coke as a deposit on my future retainer. The problem was where they figured I would sell it or use it over the next few weeks, I consumed it in a weekend and wanted more! That plan ended abruptly and not peacefully.

Years later, I found another community. In this instance, I was working as a Probation Officer for the Juvenile Court. I had a few rehab stays under my belt by this time and would be in and out of sobriety somewhat regularly. I was a Southside/Downtown guy, but found that I could disappear into a very rough neighborhood on the Westside to do my crime and drugs. My mind could rationalize anything at that time. I would disappear into the projects and dilapidated row-houses for days at a time, burning through my paycheck and then anything I could smuggle out of my house or steal from tradesman trucks and construction sites. I can recall one morning walking down a dirty rat-infested alley as the Sun started to rise; I was alone, because my money had run out and the last rock had been smoked. So, as I wandered the streets waiting for the next opportunity to find anything of value, I said to myself, "There's nothing wrong here, some people go on vacation to Disney World. I just choose to spend my time and money like this." In this ridiculous instance, I had a community. There were several people that were willing to be my ghetto tour guides, as long as I was paying for the dope. I had a negative community of support.

The Recovery Community in Rockford

When I moved to Rockford, IL in 2008, I was really flying blind. I had only driven through the town previously, so I really didn't know what to expect. I moved into a sober house in a pretty bad neighborhood on the west side of town and tried to get comfortable. This wasn't my first go round in a sober house or getting back on the wagon, so I already knew what had to be done. I needed to go to as many meetings as I could, get swallowed up by the Big Book, try to determine which of my housemates were "safe" to hang out with and get a job quickly. Oh, and in my mind, I had to find a girl... I had deduced that I relapsed because of my last relationship break up, so I figured finding a replacement would keep me on the right track. That was my universe.

I have to admit that I really wasn't connecting with the guys in the Rockford house. As someone that had already experienced long-term recovery, it was hard to not come off as a know-it-all. I had been **"dry"** for 14 years prior to my relapse event. I remember condescendingly scoffing when one of the guys couldn't read "How It Works"in the AA Big Book. How can you go to a meeting every day for months and hear the same reading, but when it comes to you, it's like you're reading ancient Hebrew? I was so full of myself. The truth is, I thought I was better than these guys. And it showed... (not like arrogance hasn't proven to be a problem for me before).

As luck would have it, I got a job pretty quickly and a car followed shortly after. With those two covered, I was able to attend meetings outside of the walking distance limit I had been subject to at the house. Rockford was a terrific place to get sober back then. It was a town of 180,000 people with about 350 AA meetings weekly. There were 12 step clubs that met a variety of appetites; the club that had weekly activities and huge meetings, the Big Book Thumper meeting, the meeting house for the homeless and destitute, as well as the fanatic sponsor meetings that were invite only. I ended up finding a meeting that I liked right across the street from the restaurant where I worked. It was a larger meeting than I was used to attending, with around 40+ people every weekday for the noon meeting. I really don't know why I got attached to that meeting so quickly. In fact, I had reason not to. The first time I tried to attend a meeting there, I arrived after the meeting ended. An older white gentleman that thought he was being helpful met me. I told him a little about my situation and that I didn't have a sponsor yet. I remember him telling me that I would like the group and find a sponsor because "there's quite a few black guys that attend the meetings here..." I remember wondering if this guy thought only native Americans could sponsor indigenous people and the same for Asians, LatinX and so on. Whatever...

So I started attending the noon meeting every day. The tables were set up in a giant U and I found a seat on one side that I liked. There was a group of old-timers that sat across from me every day in the same seats. Between the 6 people, they had almost 250 years of sobriety. I started to think of them as a line of angels. They became my reference team. When I was trying to make a decision, I asked myself how Chuck, Patti, Jo, Nancy, Dale and Ron would react to it. Dale had a vague likeness to my image of God. He was an 80 year old white man with longer stark white hair, bald on the top and a crisp white trimmed beard. I ended up asking him to sponsor me and he agreed. You often hear that you should pick a sponsor that has something you want. In my case, I needed a sponsor that I could give some reverence to.

I learned so much from the people in that group. While the sober house trusted us about as far as they could throw us, the group at Healthy Solutions immediately gave me a key to the front door. I remember buying a special keyring for my 1 and only key. I took that gesture as a sign that my life was rebuilding. I was super broke at the time I started chairing meetings and got in the habit of holding on to the group collection from my meetings until payday, after which I'd place it in the deposit vault. As you can imagine, eventually I got out of synch and owed the group about $50. A wonderful woman named Patti approached me without judgement or animosity and asked if I had the money. When I admitted that I didn't, she didn't threaten me with exclusion or embarrassment. She simply stated that she was disappointed, but she understood. We worked out a repayment plan and moved on. It was one of the most loving things to happen to me and she and I are friends to this day, 17 years later.

Our stigma is unfair, unwarranted and undeserved, but it is not unimaginable. We are not always well adjusted, well mannered or well behaved. As it is said that we stop growing emotionally when we start using illicit substances, we often do not grow in our social skills. We also come with myriad co-occurring mental health issues that can cloud our engagement with the world. Put simply, it can be hard for the "normal" world to understand and interact with people experiencing addiction issues to substances, behaviors like eating, overspending or other co-occurring mental health issues. In my position with the RCO, I frequently help people find employment. I often have to counsel the employers prior to hiring that they will need a new approach with a person in very early recovery. Early recovery is a time of constant change, seemingly whimsical and abrupt life decisions and the ever-present risk of relapse. When an individual in early recovery is doing well, they will be prioritizing their "program" above their employment. However, when they are struggling, it will impact their work as well. There are 1000 ways that early recovery paints itself upon a person and pushes them outside of the mainstream. Everything from finding employment and housing to interpersonal relationships can be harder to come by and maintain. Often, the recovery community is the one place that person can exist without the stigma.

Eventually, early recovery turns into long-term recovery. Those people that are lucky enough to make it to that classification often have a soft spot for people coming up behind them. In most places, there are a few contractors or business owners that are part of the group and will offer immediate, come-as-you-are employment. Most meetings have a network that can help a newbie find an apartment or a cheap vehicle. This is the safety of the group in action. The group is shielding the newcomer from the negativity of the world and its judgment. No one with less than 90 days clean needs to face multiple and sustained rejections and failure. This is what we are used to. By leaning on the recovery community, the newcomer can experience small successes and form their own personal support system in a more sympathetic world.

Code Switching as a Way of Life

I returned to Chicago after college in 1988. Back in my home town, I quickly found my own friends and tried to pick up like I'd been here all along. I also learned that I had to live in many social planes and each required me to present a little differently. I had a professional face, so I could try to maintain a job; I had a "cool guy" face for the ladies (actually, I had an idiot face that I thought was cool, but not as many ladies as I would have liked). I had my streetwise face and my adorable face, and I could shift on a dime.

I'm talking about code switching. I liken myself to a professional code switcher, the ability to present oneself in a variety of affects that are designed to better fit into the present situation. I am a chameleon when it comes to this. I wish I could tell you whether this is a good thing or not. My militant black brothers will say that I sell out when I "talk white" and take the swag out of my step. I don't know what my bosses at work say about my neighborhood dialect and behavior, because it gets me shut out of a lot of conversations.

There are significant benefits to this ability to adapt to different situations. It allows for a very diverse set of life experiences and opens up the world, not only socially, but geographically. It is also one of the first defenses one learns. OK, here we go…. My real name is Gaylloyd. I don't know what a baby can do to piss a new mother off so bad that she thinks that name will be a good idea, but I'm a junior, so at least 2 mothers in a row did this to a child. What does this have to do with code switching? I am literally 2 people at all times. Imagine what 4th grade kids do to a kid with the name Gaylloyd… I couldn't avoid it at school because the teachers would read it at attendance and inevitably call me "Gaylord". But the kids at home and in the neighborhood had to ask my name. I told them Gerald.

So Gaylloyd exists at school and in places where my legal name will be used. You have to just own a name like that. You stand as tall as you can, learn to crack back on anyone trying to make fun of you and present to the world like the name comes of a royal lineage. I will not show weakness. I will not let them know … Funny thing is that now, as an adult, I kind of like having this alter ego. When bill collectors or spam salesmen call, they ask for Gaylloyd. He's never home...

I prefer the name Gerald. There is a long story about a friend of my parents named Gerald that I was to be named after, but my mother feared my dad having children out of wedlock. She didn't want anyone else to be named as his junior so she claimed the name "Gaylloyd, Junior". Being Gerald was fun; family and friends from the neighborhood all called me by that name. In fact, my Mom and Dad called me by that name, but technically, Gerald doesn't exist. Throughout my life, I have hung a great many tags on the name, some good, some bad.

Gerald is who I am today. Sometime during my 30s, my father pulled me aside and told me that he wouldn't be insulted if I legally changed my name. It was a nice gesture, but I wish he'd expressed this 25 years earlier, when I was getting massacred on the school playground. At this point, I don't think it matters anymore. My signature is Gerald. If it is something that is semi-legal, I use "G. Gerald " and when I know it is a true legal document, I sign "Gaylloyd". This can sometimes lead to multiple levels of code switching all at the same time! Talk about a confusing mess.

For someone like me, code switching to this extent can be extremely dangerous. "Someone like me" meaning a person with an addictive personality and creative mind easily gets lost in the switches and sometimes I have a hard time finding my way back to who I really am. I tell myself stories and I start to believe them. I wonder if maybe Gerald is an addict and alcoholic, but Gaylloyd is not.

For someone like me, it is really easy to completely BS a support meeting. I am very used to having multiple "truths". I can sit in a meeting and contort my personality to be appropriate. The very next day I can be out whooping it up with my drunk buddies at the strip club. In both situations, I will be entirely comfortable with no regret or remorse regarding the other. In my mind, the other side doesn't exist at that moment. This is the essence of code switching. It is also a mechanism for addiction. I can compartmentalize the damage of a binge as a "unfortunate mishap", inconsequential to the entirety of my life. This mental gymnastics comes with a side order of "how's it hurting anyone else anyway?".

Belonging to multiple groups is how I fight against this. Preferably, multiple groups with overlapping members. Code switching only really works when the people you encounter are separate and distinct parts of your life. It's very hard to change your behavior in front of people without them noticing and saying something about it. As my groups merge and overlap, I connot present different faces as easily. The group becomes my "lie detector".

My Work Tribe

They say that today's generation doesn't like to work. I find that every generation thinks the ones that come after them are lazy, good for nothing losers. If I am honest, I know I'm no amazing worker. What I am is lonely. I like being with my co-workers. I spend more time with them than I do with my family. We have common goals and experiences and share a mission. So I don't know if I am coming to work because I want to be productive or because that is where my people are.

I am at my desk by 7:30am and don't leave until after 5. I am happy to work extra hours or events or to sit on the phone for hours with a peer. My work is my life and my family is aware of this priority. I love going to conferences, symposiums and conventions. That is where I can see just how big our tribe is. We that do the work. What work you may ask? It doesn't matter. When I was in the auto dealership, I loved those outings. Now that I am in the recovery game, I still love those. I love any chance to see people from far away that do what I do.

Some might say my work habits aren't healthy. They may say I am a workaholic that has traded one addiction for another. I could not counter the accusation. I certainly find myself asking more of my team than they probably want to give. In my mind, our work is similar to other tribes I have been a member of; it is a 24-hour identity that doesn't take time off. I think of policemen. Yes, they may have days off, but they are still considered policemen and as a result, are always required to act in the event of an emergency. It is not "what they do", it is "who they are". This is my outlook. I am my work. I find that the world supports this delusion, in that most introductions are shortly thereafter followed by, "So what do you do?" Knowing my name and that we are at the intersection of our lives (a party, a sporting event or some other social setting) isn't enough; the other party wants to rank me. If I say I am a doctor, I go in one pile. If I say I am a traveling salesman, I will be placed in another category. The hierarchy of categories is within the questioner. In some settings, a doctor ranks high; in others, the good doctor might be a pariah.

I push myself very hard to achieve. My work tribe are the people that help me on this mission. Of all my tribes, this is the most confusing one, because it is wholly transactional. In most of my other groups, the members are there because they have innate qualities or life circumstances that create commonality. In work, it is really just a random occurrence of who is employed at the XYZ Company. Unless you have the privilege of starting a company, running it without oversight and building your workforce through selective recruiting, you have a random grouping based on several factors. Workforces are made up of who is available, interested then applies, and is hired. From there, I must build my tribe. Anyone that has been employed knows that there are always people that see work as less of a priority than others. There are people that stay a short time and others that stay for the long haul. I prefer to stay for as long as I can. I like being one of the pillars of the organization with time under my belt.

The work tribe gets super confusing to me when people's motivations change. I guess this is true with all groups, but I see it most in this environment. I have already discussed my difficulty in understanding people. Here is a kick; as an addict/hustler, I can "read" people well enough to sell them ideas and items. As a person, I am completely lost in interpersonal relationships. The closeness of the work environment can often be a tight container, where I along with my co-workers mix into nitroglycerine. Boom!

The work tribe is unique because of the transience of the members. In all my other tribes, people are there because they want to be. In the work tribe, there are members who are only there because of the paycheck. And no other "tribe" has the formality of coming and going as in hiring and firing. It is often difficult to know who is part of the tribe and who is just around. Also, can someone be part of the work tribe but work for a different employer—like the guy across the hall that you see every day and chat with at the coffee stand downstairs? As I write this, I am getting anxious and have just decided that I am taking tomorrow off!

What is the Alternative?

This book has suggested that the most effective way for communities to support people in recovery is to help them come together as a universal support system. For decades, we have tried policing people into good behavior using shame and ostracization, talk therapy and countless other strategies. Some of those tactics are just flat out cruel, while others have merit as "part" of a system. Like chapters in a book, they only bear fruit when consumed in context with their other components. Recovery is such a "book".

As I have discussed, I presently live in a very small rural town. Our small piece of the planet is located about 100 miles due west of Chicago. Here, approximately 60,000 people live in 3 conjoined towns. My town, Dixon, is best known for a woman embezzling $50,000,000 and ironically, as the boyhood home of Ronald Reagan, father of the "War on Drugs". I am very proud of my team's efforts to see the drug problem compassionately, as opposed to that draconian legal catastrophe (but that is for another book). In our towns, the stigma of substance use disorder is all too real. Here in small-town America where everyone knows one another, history doesn't die quickly. People remember who was a problem back in high school, whose family got evicted because dad was drunk and who was driving on that terrible night when things turned ugly.

Once a person has been dressed by the community in the "Damaged" suit, it is extremely difficult to take it off. Small towns often have the effect of pushing people that enter recovery back into the mold of their old self. Consider a person that grew up here in a family known to have issues with the law and substance abuse. People probably said the son is destined to follow in the father's footsteps. When that child does eventually make a mistake, it's not seen as an outlier, but as the inevitable. Instead of him then rising from it, the incident becomes the anchor for the sad story that is his life. One mistake after another is piled up in the minds of the community until he becomes the fulfillment of the prophecy. He is not offered jobs that can lift him. He is not welcomed into groups that are moving upward. He finds his society and camaraderie among the other discarded souls. Eventually, he finds the relief of drugs and we know where that can lead, but here is the moment of truth: If that person can find his way into recovery. Let's say he goes away to treatment for 28 days and then to a sober living house for a few months. What happens when he returns? Does the community give him a fresh start? Do they say bygones are bygones and offer him a high paying and respected position? No. The community immediately begins to push him back into the role he played prior. While he is trying to establish a new way of life, he is fighting a community that still wants to see him as the previous man. He tries to gain employment, he tries to socialize, he may even try to volunteer and give back. However, it will be all to no avail, as the community only sees him as the problem child of a problem father. It takes a very long time for society to recognize good behavior and attribute that to true and earnest change. There is also the "no man is a saint" aspect. Though our fellow might do 1000 things right, if he makes but 1 public mistake, it can all come crumbling down. Please recall that our subject is in very early recovery. There is very little emotional resilience and toughness. This is a moment when many succumb to frustration. "If they're gonna see me as bad anyway, I might as well …"

The alternative for thousands of people is to remain alone. With no one to reinforce their new ideals and little positive feedback, they are their own first and last defense against sliding back into their old character. Many people think that substance use disorders are a failure of one's moral system. As a recovering alcoholic/addict, I say that my morals never failed; it was my thinking that was faulty. My mind gave me erroneous messages that reinforced behaviors that were to my own detriment. This is critical because I cannot be expected to chart a path out of a problem while my mind subconsciously continues to create it. Alone, I am my own victim.

I was once taught about the agreements that hold society together. Every person has hundreds of agreements going on at the same time at all times. We all agree that the red octagonal street sign means I should stop. We all agree not to lash out violently at strangers because we are upset by minor things. These are passive agreements that most people abide by or face some penalty from the group. What is interesting about agreements is the ones we are willing to break. Generally, as the agreement partner becomes closer to us, we are more willing to break agreements with them. This is because we feel we can dodge or alter the consequences more with people that we are in close relationships with. Consider the domestic abuser that is violent with their family, but would never raise a hand outside the house. He knows his wife will accept his apology (for the 100th time) but he has no confidence people outside his home will give the same grace.

There is no one closer to a person than the individual themselves. We all have agreements with ourselves. Those are the hardest to keep. Think of how many times you have sworn to change a behavior - dieting, not drinking, not checking the social media posts of an ex-romantic partner. I can speak to this personally. I have made agreements with myself with regard to fitness for the last 40 years. At present, I have told myself that I will do 50 push-ups every day for 30 days. Day One - I do 25. I tell myself it is because I am out of shape. Day Two - 30. I rationalize that I don't have a lot of time, so I have to work harder in the future. Day Three - 30. This is harder than I thought, but I will catch up by doing extra in the future. Jump to Day Fifteen - so far, I have only done 50 push-ups in a day twice. I have broken my agreement with myself. My consequence for this failure is nothing. I let myself off the hook. If I can't hold myself to a simple 30-day push-up discipline, the odds are severely stacked that I cannot "just decide" to stop drinking or using drugs. This is where I lean on the power of my social groups and tribes. I may not hold agreements with myself, but I almost always hold them with others, especially large groups that I value and want to remain in good standing with. In my many years of sobriety, I can honestly admit that there have been times when I wanted to give in and start drinking, but I didn't because I feared losing my status with the recovery group. That was my only fence I wouldn't cross. I have let myself down and I know that I will eventually forgive myself. I don't have that same confidence in my tribes.

Alcoholics Anonymous speaks of the point where an alcoholic is left with only 2 choices; to go on to the bitter end or accept the help provided by God and the 12 steps. This is true of every path to recovery. You either choose to walk the path or stay in the disease. However, there is another choice that is presented later in recovery. That choice is either I give myself over to a new life or I suffer without my "solution". The new life will present any number of new opportunities and life branches out in 100 new directions. The "suffering" is to try to hang on to attachments formed prior to my recovery, but look at them through my new "dry" eyes. What we find is loneliness, longing and misery as one comes to the realization that that life is custom made to fit exactly one person, your "using" self. True recovery is found when a person accepts that some of the previous life will not make it into the new one. There is no rule as to what will make the cut, but addiction impacts every part of a person's life and sometimes it cannot be reversed.

Ask any group of people in recovery what they have given up for their recovery and you will hear stories of failed marriages, jobs quit and friendships abandoned. This shouldn't come as a surprise. It is always easier (in theory) to cut something out of your life than to add something. I have been trying to add working out to my schedule to lose weight. I have found it much easier to cut down on carbonated sugar drinks. In recovery, the add-ons are even more difficult. Putting down my shield of drink or drug is an invitation to the uncomfortable pain I seek to avoid. I add meetings or therapy, but the pain is still there. There is no avoiding the truth that life is hard and hurts.

Affinity Groups

We've all seen the movie where a man and a woman are essentially strangers at the beginning and then some crisis comes along; the earth opens up and starts swallowing buildings; dinosaurs come back in 1980; an airplane falls out of the sky on top of them, whatever the crisis, they have to go through an hour and a half of running around together, trying to save one another and by the end of the movie, they're in love. This is a crisis relationship. A trope that we all know is people, even enemies, who experience tough things together, become closer. What bigger crisis is there than addiction and trying to get into recovery? It can be the single most defining thing about a person. With all bridges burned, I walk into recovery alone with only my disaster. Generally, and even when there is compassion, our friends and family are at the end of their patience. If you are under the impression that the using/drinking streets are full of genuine love and connection, you are wrong. The tail end of an addiction is filled with judgment, fear, shame and loneliness. There is nothing more demoralizing than being in a room of low-bottom, criminal, emaciated and filthy junkies and they look at you and say "Man, you're in too deep. You need to get some help." - "Really, Fuck You! Did I need help when I took $800 out of my mother's ATM and bought drugs for the house last week?" The answer - "No." But that was last week...

So I walk into recovery, that moment when I finally admit that I have to do something about my problem, with nothing but the unbreakable cage around my mind that is my addiction, its accompanying stigma and whatever horrible thing that I am enduring and want to numb. I just need someone else around to do that with me, and while I don't think that addiction is good by any stretch of the imagination, I think it often rises to the level of crisis sufficient to make people bond in those extreme ways. Perhaps the difference is that your addiction is generally a lifelong problem you've been dealing with. Whereas in the movie style emergency, where on Sunday everything is good, on Monday, pterodactyls are eating children from the local park. It's sudden, surprising and exotic. Addiction is a slow process that has been tearing away at a person and their loved ones for a long time. When I was out using drugs, even though I had a $400 a day crack habit, I would look down on people that used drugs. I remember calling them "hypes" and saying how I didn't wanna be around people like that even though I was people like that. So the notion that we're all in the same boat together and we're growing towards recovery from addiction, is shattered. People in addiction see themselves as different and unique. Around 12 step rooms, we sometimes hear people say that addicts and alcoholics see themselves as "terminally unique". My addiction puts me on the outside of everything. So when I meet people and develop a bond of sorts because we are entering recovery alongside one another, I want to say we'll be together for the long haul. My hope is that I have finally found the missing piece for which I have been searching. WE are in recovery together. Thinking that this fact alone is going to keep us together is patently false. Truth is, most of the people I met in rehabs and my early meetings have faded into memories long ago. Where you would expect people in recovery to logically recognize that this new group of peers is beneficial to them and that they should nurture and value the connections, in fact it's just the opposite. In many instances, I, as the person entering new recovery, want to get as far away from the people that share my plight. People just in from the proverbial cold aren't always ready for the recovery mindset. They enter a meeting hall and hear people laughing. They wonder if the joke is on them. They see people sharing intimate life details and wonder if anyone is looking to use their information against them. They hear the Steps and Traditions and it brings up fears of studying and school age anxiety. We have heard from many newcomers that they don't like going to 12 step meetings because "it's just a bunch of people complaining about life. I translate that to "I find nothing there to relate or aspire to". What is different about sitting around a table and allowing misery to overtake me. Either way, I am alone with my demons.

Here is where we find an opportunity to take a new direction. What if we can find a way to build the connection without focusing on the problem? If the newcomer cannot bring themselves to face their issue head on, perhaps they can participate in some other activity with people that share the same background. I reference The Phoenix Sober Activity Community again. We have hosted Phoenix events for 2 years and have found their strategy to be effective. Our most successful Phoenix program is our weekly pick-up basketball. We have seen people that are hard pressed to attend a support meeting show up religiously to play basketball. In that scenario there is zero pressure to delve into the "why" of my addiction or the pain of life's struggles. Of course there are times when everyone is sitting on a bench between games and the question is asked, "How are you holding up with regard to your drinking?" That is the magic. Suddenly the guest spills his truth. He is struggling or he is doing fantastic. Either way, the conversation has started in a non-threatening, comfortable way. We have seen many of our basketball attendees go on to take further steps towards involvement in the recovery community as speakers and volunteers at our recovery focused events.

There are as many reasons as not that people don't feel they fit into 12 step recovery meetings. The "Anonymii" are very specific situations in which one is first required to take the seal off deeply covered traumas and reflect the topics of discussion off them. Then they have to make space for the idea that the solution to these troubles can be found in God. Then they have to accept that even though God can fix their lives and it is painfully obvious that such repair is needed, God will only do so if they carry out a set of 12 actions. After all this, they still are not guaranteed everlasting sobriety and peace. That will only come if they 1) want it enough and 2) admit that they will never "finish" doing the work to obtain it. To a mind seeking immediate answers to age old problems, this doesn't sound like a good plan. I, as a drug user and alcoholic, have spent entirely too much time and energy figuring out how to avoid responsibility and emotional work. I need something that allows me to start building fellowship without the threat of being forced to bear my scars.

Tribe finding in our context is entering long-term recovery through recovery-based, but not focused, social groups. The glue of these groups is not the trauma and chaos of our addiction, but the growth of a positive interest. These are groups that acknowledge the substance use disorder as opposed to a separate gathering that the person seeking recovery uses as a distraction. I often hear of people that say they have found a replacement activity like working out, church groups or sports league and that as long as they are occupied by those, they do not seek out their substance of choice. Our issue comes in the fact that relapse- as a process over time- often goes unnoticed in these groups. In some instances, it is noticed and because other members of the group don't share the affliction, it becomes a reason to put distance between the person and the group. So as I applaud people that find positive ways to spend time and energy in early recovery, I must state that joining the local tennis league may not be the answer. The answer is to join the "recovery tennis" league. There one will find the empathy, camaraderie and support that will respond appropriately to their condition.

I have previously discussed the commonality of most paths to recovery. We (the group) are brought together by our affliction and that is what we all have in common. My "yuck" is my admission ticket. As random people from all walks of life assemble around a table, their connection point is that part of them that they hope to excise. If I am lucky, strong, faithful or diligent, I start to get better. My addiction will get smaller in my life and that is what I would have in common with this group. As new people come in, I'd start to notice that I don't relate as well to them. Due to the fact that my relapse after 14 years happened in Spring, I didn't use during the holidays. If you add the 14 years to the present 17 years of sobriety, I haven't had to struggle with the "Thanksgiving/Christmas is hard to stay sober" issue in 3 decades. The holidays aren't really a problem for me with regard to my substance use. Every year as I am sitting in my early November AA meetings, a newcomer will bring up the topic saying, "I don't know how I am going to make it through the family Christmas dinner." I feel my eyes roll as I hold back a snicker and condescendingly think of how simple the solution is. "Just don't go!" I mutter to myself and immediately I have broken the bond of support. We are no longer equals and our attachment to the group has diminished as well. The newcomer can no longer feel safe in sharing his struggles and I have demonstrated my inability to respect my peer's situation as being important to them. This is a critical moment for the group. This is the point where one or both of the two members may shear off. The newcomer leaves because he or she is not finding sufficient compassion to feel safe in expressing his or her struggle or the old-timer leaves because the belief is that the group is no longer challenging their primary issues. The point of participation in affinity groups is to find accountability partners in a social network that holds sobriety (or recovery as a spectrum) as an expectation, and focus is not on the length or vesting of recovery in the individual, but the growth of the affinity subject.

When it comes to recovery, I must submit that Alcoholics Anonymous saved my life. I one hundred percent believe in the 12-step program for recovery. I offer up affinity groups as a supplement, not a replacement. Nevertheless, there are people who will never give AA or any of the 12 step groups a try. They may attend, they may sit through a meeting and they may tell you they've read the literature, the fact is they are not gonna give it a shot due to childhood and/or other trauma, which keeps them from opening up. They may fear big groups, have issues, which make them distrustful of people, fear speaking in public or any other number of reasons. The end result is the same. They need a way to join society without the structure of a 12 step meeting or its value system. For these people, we have found several alternative options. As I mentioned earlier, In the last couple of years, I have become aware of The Phoenix Sober Activity Community, now called New Form. It utilizes the tech of today, the App, to invite people to participate in healthy activities designed to support their recovery from substance use disorders. People can search out virtual activities, pre-recorded meditations and work-outs or live in-person events in their area. The only requirement for participation is that the person is 48 hours sober at the time.

So I am defining an affinity group as any group that is organized to allow people to gather and build relationships based on some activity of mutual interest as an antidote to addiction. For our discussion, that group must have a component that offers support to people in recovery from substance use disorders and co-occurring mental health issues. The core of the concept is allowing people to congregate and build trust/fellowship without directly focusing on a problem that we know will last forever. There is no rush to tackle the addiction issue if the person is not actively using, so we allow it to rest while we build community and systems of support.

I was recently granted a tour of Hope Recovery Community in Medina, OH. As a RCO, they offer all the usual recovery paths - 12 step, SMART, meditation etc. What caught my attention was out in the garage. It's called Motorcycle Rehab. Backstory - Hope is a motorcycle-culture recovery organization. By that, I mean its leaders are motorcycle enthusiasts and their big annual fundraising event is a motorcycle run that yields them $50,000+ every year! They know bikes. Apparently, a few of their peers found or were gifted a bike frame and they started trying to make something of it. They approached the Hope team and asked for support. Hope purchased tools, a lift and underwrote parts for them. The result of that assistance is a group of people that meet every Saturday to work on the project bike and talk. They have formed a cohesive unit around the task, not their impediments. In the end, the completed bike is raffled off, with proceeds going toward buying a new frame and the rest going back to the Hope organization to restart the process. Bonus - a couple of the guys realized they needed to know how to weld, so they enrolled in a certificate program at the local community college. They are now certified welders working in the trade.

I love the Motorcycle Rehab program. It aligns with my ideas of how to welcome people into our community. Throughout my sober journey, I have met people that are so impacted by their new sobriety that it becomes their one and only discussion topic. I can recall telling people that they don't have to actively recover 24 hours a day. Every decision, thought and action does not have to be focused on getting sober. Generally, whenever I encounter people in this state, I find that they burn out rather quickly and become completely turned off from recovery. I don't see the goal being to burn the brightest; I want to burn longer in my recovery. Programs like Motorcycle Rehab are perfect for this mindset. Members of the group gather regularly with a set of tasks and goals that are not dependent upon their mental state. A motorcycle frame waiting for installation of a motor could care less if I, the installer, am in a good mood. I have seen this theory play out in some prison programs that allow inmates to work with animals. The animals don't judge the prisoner's past, but react to the care they receive in the moment. In Motorcycle Rehab, the rank and status of members is not contingent upon how long they have been sober or whether they have experienced a relapse. As the build proceeds, a person's skill at welding, painting or electrical wiring will take precedence. Your relative value to the group and project is based on your skillset and willingness to apply yourself. There is a freedom in this, because often, people entering more traditional recovery support groups feel they are marginalized as "newbies". Old-timers tell them to be quiet and just listen like they have nothing of value to offer. In affinity groups like Motorcycle Rehab, membership is based on a factor that the individual can control unlike their substance use disorder; they are members because of their love of the subject/activity/project.

If you are active in your local recovery scene or if your recovery status is known, you probably have a few "Referrers". These are people that associate you with "Getting Better" and direct random people to you for mentoring. One of my referrers, who I will call Steve, is a good guy that works in the field. He has been around for a long time and I believe he is excited to know there is someone in the community that wants to help. Every month, I get one or two calls from people saying they were told to call me, by Steve. My question is always the same, "What did he tell you to ask of me?" They never know. I am not sure if he is not telling them or they are not listening. Whatever the reason, they seem to be looking for an entry way into recovery. They seem to want someone to spark something in them that makes it all make sense. I wish I could say that I have the answer, but I don't. Unfortunately a short phone conversation with someone doesn't seem to be enough to grab them and create the attachment. They need to fully commit to a lifestyle change that is not only satisfying enough to soothe the demons that lead to addiction, but also creates the hope to move forward. So far, I have not seen one person be that agent of change.

I have, however, seen "Referrers" find success when they refer people to groups. "You should come to my Home Group, I will take you and introduce you" or "You should check out the group that meets on Thursdays at the Church, they are very active in community service." Here, the referral is based on more than just the need for help. These referrals go a step further, in that they associate a characteristic to which the subject of the referral may attach i.e. "very active in community service" (because you said you want to give back). These referrals also have the benefit of spreading the responsibility of being a role model over a group, rather than an individual. I believe that our opportunities to engage people into recovery at the early stages of sobriety are limited. Remember, failure equals a return to active use. Therefore, I am well aware that when that person calls, they are looking for me to say that "Thing". You know, the statement that sums up life and tells them it's time to make the change. The proverbial street lights coming on that signaled to us as children that it was time to go home. That is a lot of pressure for one person who probably got the surprise call while walking the aisles of their local grocery store.

The referral to the group has much less pressure. The statement was not "call this guy, he will make it make sense…" but "connect with this group, you will find something positive there…"

This is the heart of Affinity Group Recovery. It is the admission that people are flawed and subjective. I cannot hang the weight of my recovery on any one person. Doing so will require that person to become a deity. They cannot be late, cannot make mistakes, cannot show flaws and cannot say the wrong thing or they risk driving their mentee away from themselves and the promise of recovery. The group on the other hand comes with many personalities and abilities. As the group focuses on the external motif, be it music, athletics or art, the individuals learn to trust and rely on one another. In the rock climbing group, there is no pressure to immediately share your private struggles, fears or failures. That can come at the top of the rock as the members relax in the afternoon sun. The primary push of the group is to engage in the activity.

My Home Group Tribe

I think anyone reading this book is aware that I found recovery via Alcoholics Anonymous. For me, my home group is the most important component of my AA experience. I have tried to do AA where I bounce from group to group and never really allow anyone to know exactly who I am or what I am facing. That didn't work. Today I am a steady and consistent member of 1 group. That group knows me. We speak outside of meetings, we generally will notify the group if we are going to miss a meeting and we share a belief in the way we do AA.

That last part is most important. There are many different ways that people exercise the 12 step program. Some people believe the secret sauce is the fellowship; others want to work the steps exactly like the book details. Then there are others that think that AA is something one does for a short time until you get "better". My thinking on how to do AA is irrelevant and only matters to me. If people can find their definition of recovery success in some of these ways, I salute them. What I know to be fact is - you have to find a group that does AA in the way that makes sense to you. I am aware of some really strict, almost militant, groups. That style of recovery just would not work for me.

My home group is pretty laid back, but we lean towards long-term sobriety. On any given Wednesday, we will have 10-14 people with an average sobriety length of 20+ years. Our topics come from the Big Book or other AA approved books. We are pretty strict about keeping to the topic and not cross-talking. Other than that, we are any average group. I love being a part of this group in this community. I mark that as important, because I don't know that it would be the same if I still lived in a large city like Chicago. My present group, New Solutions, has just enough members, so much that I see people from the group around town pretty regularly. I bump into them at the grocery store and see them in church. I need to know that my recovery isn't just something that happens while I am sitting at the meeting table. My recovery is a community and those people are in my life in multiple ways. The beauty of the lengthy sobriety times is that most of these people hardly identify as primarily being in recovery any longer. When I bump into them at the gas station, the conversation isn't about drinking or not. We talk about the news, the weather and how horrible the Chicago Bears are this and every year. These are people that I am proud of and happy to know. As I see them out in the world making a difference for the positive, I also see myself.

The 12 Step Solution is a Path to Healthy Socialization

The 12 steps also known to many as the "Anonymous" groups represent a program that relies on socialization and people working together. Let's not even go to the "meetings" part of it. In actuality, The Big Book of Alcoholics Anonymous never defines what a "meeting" is in the first 164 pages, which is the instructive section of the book. It is not until you get into the stories that you read about "meetings" as we know them today. But at every step along the road to recovery, the reader is reminded that they will need to be supported by and be a support to others. In fact, the whole point of the 12th step is to share what has been found with others.

In Step 5 -(Admitted to God, to ourselves and to another human being the exact nature of our wrongs). We are told that it is our reflection in the eyes of another that shows truth. The book specifically discusses what the knowledge of one's moral inventory yields in the absence of an outside opinion. "In actual practice, we usually find a solitary self-appraisal insufficient. Many of us thought it necessary to go much further. We will be more reconciled to discussing ourselves with another person when we see good reasons why we should do so. The best reason first: if we skip this vital step, we may not overcome drinking. Time after time, newcomers have tried to keep to themselves certain facts about their lives. Trying to avoid this humbling experience, they have turned to easier methods. Almost invariably, they got drunk. Having persevered with the rest of the program, they wondered why they fell. We think the reason is that they never completed their housecleaning. They took inventory all right, but hung on to some of the worst items in stock. They only thought they had lost their egoism and fear; they only thought they had humbled themselves, but they had not learned enough about humility, fearlessness and honesty, in the sense we find it necessary, until they told someone else all of their life story." – AA Big Book - Page 72 . Plainly stated, when people in recovery keep their troubles secret, they tend to become reasons to return to drinking/drug use.

In Step 9 - (Made direct amends to such people wherever possible, except when to do so would injure them or others) - we again see that the 12 step process puts you on a direct intersection course with others. As a spiritual journey, the 12 steps seek to right-size the individual in relation to God and to other people. The "amends" step requires the participant to seek out those in their past with whom relations have been threatened and to resolve those issues. A successful mending of the relationship does not necessarily precede a re-initiation of the connection, but it seeks to tear down any barriers to such. I was once told by a sponsor that I would know when I needed to make amends to someone because I would want to duck down another aisle if I bumped into them at the grocery store.

Step 12 - (Having had a spiritual awakening as the result of these steps, we tried to carry this message to alcoholics, and to practice these principles in all our affairs) - directly points the newly recovered to the man standing behind him in line. There is no disputing that one of the major benefits of the 12 step doctrine is that we cannot recover in isolation and thus, those seeking wellness are unequivocally forced out into society. If the main problem of the alcoholic, as stated in the book, is selfishness and self-centeredness, the solution is obvious, the person has to become more altruistic and sharing. Therefore, AA and the 12 steps are less about stopping the destructive drinking and more about realigning with society so as not to require the courage, safety, numbness, etc. that the alcoholic finds in their substance use and needs in order to interact with his fellows.

As I stated earlier, there is no directive in the "Program" section (the first 164 pages that are the voice of the original Authors) of the Big Book that requires one to attend organized meetings on a regular basis. That fact exists even though the nature of the entire system is built on helping people return to the mainstream of society. There is a saying in AA, "Meeting makers make it..." While I have my issues with breaking such a complex program into bite-sized slogans that are so easily misunderstood, I see what they are trying to say. The meeting/fellowship is the glue that holds people in orbit of the redeeming concepts. We know that generally, people drift from structured and disciplined lifestyles toward less restrictive ways of living. Few, if any, soldiers continue the regimen they accept in basic training for the rest of their lives. Some may continue to make their bed in military fashion or to wake before sunrise, but do they force themselves out onto the obstacle course or undertake multiple mile hikes carrying full gear? Of course not. Likewise, we see people drift from the structure of treatment facilities upon their return to home life in many ways. 12 step meetings serve to help reinforce the new lifestyle of recovery by creating social pressure on the individual to continue the values and practices in their everyday lives. The idea of "practicing these principles in all our affairs" directs the 12-stepper to take the ideas of tolerance, open-mindedness, honesty and compassion out into their everyday lives. Another characteristic of those in addiction is isolation and separation from the rest of the community. Often times, the meeting rooms are the first opportunity a person entering recovery has to create new relationships in their sober lifestyle.

As with any social group, it can be very difficult for one to integrate and assimilate without instruction. This is where the "Sponsor" comes in. Again, there is no direct reference to a "Sponsor" in the first 164 pages. When you think about it, the sponsor role has existed since day one of man. None of us are born knowing how to live in this world. From the original sponsor, "Mom", who instructed us how to find sustenance, to the guy that "sponsored" one's addiction by showing them how to smoke cocaine, weed or consume alcohol, someone has indeed shown us everything we know. In the 12 step community, the sponsor serves several purposes. They explain the values and mores of the group, they become a friendly face in a strange crowd, they communicate the "inside" info like events and happenings. The sponsor is the first and only structured relationship within the group and thus, they lend permanency and attachment. Newcomers sometimes find themselves subconsciously name-checking their sponsorship lineage as an effort to cast a similar shadow as their sponsor. This can be a good and bad proposition. It is clearly indicative of a hero worship dynamic. I applaud the newcomer that has taken recovery seriously and deliberately puts upon a pedestal someone that represents a healthy body and mind. In the same breath, I ask the sponsor where their humility has gone. If the idea of the program is that only God can help the newcomer, why is the sponsor allowing the newbie to create a "false idol" and deify the sponsor? The sponsor, in my mind, is simply someone to demonstrate and moderate the process of doing the 12 steps so that the seeker can find the relief promised. I have seen many instances where a sponsor relapses leaving their sponsee confused and discouraged. To my mind, ethical sponsorship requires the sponsor to make sure their mentee understands that everyone including the sponsor is susceptible to the disease if they lose focus on their recovery.

If ego is the problem that separates me from everyone and everybody, the 12 step Community has to be a place that one finds commonality. I remember walking into my first AA meetings in Chicago back in 1988. I had yet to find it in myself to be humble and look for the similarity in those I encountered. Instead, I saw myself as sticking out like a sore thumb. I was younger, black, smarter, dumber ... Whatever it was, I didn't fit and I didn't want to fit. How could I be of this world and admit that I had to be of it for the rest of my life? I saw old men that spoke a spiritual language I felt came from outer space. There were women that would have attracted me for all the wrong reasons except, they had turned over a new leaf. As a young man just out of college and ready to attack the world, AA did not seem like the crowd I wanted to grow into. I don't know if it was purposeful or not, but I missed the whole point. I went to a Gratitude Meeting at the Lincoln Park Alano Club in Chicago and thought I figured it all out. If you are grateful for everything, you won't drink. If you don't drink, you don't do drugs. No drugs, I'm fixed. - That went about as well as you think; in 6 months, I was high and selling my mother's VCR to a kid behind a liquor store.

So what was the deal? It was the fact that I couldn't allow myself to ask anyone for help, couldn't humble myself and say I don't know what I'm doing, because of my pride, I took a small observation and ran with it. I built an understanding of the program off bullshit and it proved to be worthless. My lazy mind took the path of least resistance, assuming I could understand what and why people were doing something, simply by observing them. It was my fear that governed me. I was afraid to approach people, I couldn't stop lying to people, I imagined they were talking negatively about me and I responded by withdrawing. I think some would say I had anxiety. I believe myself to be more candid and honest; I had lost my mind.

As I enter recovery, I no longer have the numbing protection of my chemicals. I have to experience the pain without any buffers and hope that I grow emotionally from it. I can pray to the heavens above for relief, but eventually, I have to take action. I have to extend myself so that society will attach to me. What a wonderful world it would be if I could sit in the safety and comfort of my home and have interesting and positive people audition to be my friends... No, the world doesn't work like that. I have to get out there and be uncomfortable. I have to go to the hockey game with the people from work, join a book club, engage with people at my church and join service organizations. I've been doing this for 17 years now in sobriety and I still suck at it. I catch myself knit-picking and complaining. I create distance for no reason and become judgmental. My mind does everything it can to separate me from the herd like a wolf hunting me. For me, the obligation to show face at my weekly home group meeting keeps me from isolating and helps keep me from returning to my insanity.

My home group happens to have a high percentage of members with 20+ years of sobriety. With just 17 years sober, sometimes I feel like a newcomer. As we sit around the table, I have often seen some of my old friends, and myself, get frustrated when a guy who is 30 days sober, comes in and as soon as he gets a chance, launches into telling his long, drawn out, overly dramatic story of how he changed his life, turned things around, and now he has found the answer. Of course we snicker, knowing that at 30 days, you're on a pink cloud and if you're launching into such speeches, you're not working on a program, you're just trying to convince us that you're gonna work on the program. That being said, it's not about their intent; we know that intent is always to do good, but the proof is in the actions. That's an argument for another day. Today, we're talking about why people come to the group and want to give their story in such a way. It's because they want acceptance. The general impression held by most of the world is that 12 step groups sit around telling our war stories, crying over not being able to drink anymore and enjoying hearing a bawdy tale of debauchery. Nothing could be further from the truth. In fact, at a good strong meeting, you rarely hear war stories, or oftentimes, don't hear talk of drinking at all. However, the newcomer doesn't know that and he walks in looking to quickly establish his bona fides. He wants the group to know that he is one of "us". Oftentimes, this is where the situation fails. It is often at this moment that the group reacts by correcting the newcomer, telling them that's not what we do here, letting him know "Maybe you should take the cotton out of your ears and put it in your mouth." Of course, the newcomer smiles politely. He laughs it off and says, "Yeah, you're probably right", but sometimes it's not that. Sometimes they're offended. Sometimes they feel attacked, embarrassed, humiliated and pushed to the side, and then outside. Sometimes they never come back. I'm surprised at how many times I have conversations with people in the recovery world and I hear AA bashing; I hear people saying, *"It didn't work for me or I don't get into those meetings."* I don't believe them.

I have proof that it has worked for 90 years. It has helped people, if not solved their problems. There is enough evidence as I walk into the meetings of a 12 step group, whatever society I'm dealing with. I generally have examples of people who have made this thing work. Consider someone looking to learn how to play a sport. Let's use tennis. If you want to learn how to play tennis and you walk into a building where there are tennis courts and dozens of people playing tennis, some playing well, some not, do you run away and say I don't want to learn tennis from these people or do you stay, observe, interact and learn? The answer is clear; you would stay and try to soak up as much knowledge as you can. That doesn't always happen in recovery. People come to the tables and they lay them self bear, hoping to find camaraderie, sympathy and compassion. Sometimes they find rejection and when they do, they react accordingly. Their desire to stay sober and change their lives for the better goes out the window and addiction comes roaring back saying, "See,

I told you so." We know for a fact that lonely people often find companionship in a bottle. So are they looking for a buzz? Or they are looking to not feel alone?

As someone that has tried to enter recovery several times, I believe it is foolish to expect the newcomer to create their solution. Their best thinking got them to the problem. The established recovery community owes it to the newcomer to create a welcoming entryway. We the recovered must lead the way for those seeking what we have. In the section of the AA Big Book entitled "How it Works" it is stated in the opening sentence. "Rarely have we seen a person fail who has thoroughly followed our path..." If the intention is to be followed, one must make sure that the path is obvious, obtainable and safe.

Recovery Begins

In beating my addiction, my spiritual and social recovery is my saving grace. Spiritually, I must accept that I am part of the whole. I am not the best nor the worst part; I am simply a part. Whether I look towards religion or not, I have to bring my perception of my place in the world into an accurate scale. As I do this, I find other people that are living similar lives and I can allow them the respect needed to form friendships. This begins my social recovery. As I begin to repair my tangible connections to other people, I will learn to accept their boundaries, value their input and place their needs on an even plane with my own. Eventually I start seeking new opportunities to offer something rather than demand. I become capable of being in relation with others. These skills are acquired by trial and error as I cycle through my various life segments like so many outfits on a dressing room floor.

Former Arkansas Director of Recovery and Miracle of Recovery, Jimmy McGill, talks about the 4 things needed for recovery as being community, health, home and purpose. These are the 4 Pillars of Recovery according to SAMHSA (the US Substance Abuse and Mental Health Services Administration). You will hear of these pillars in speeches, documents and books, but there is something about the way Jimmy discusses the concepts. It is not lost on me that he mentions community first. Jimmy and his lovely wife, Chelsea, created a sober living system called Next Step Recovery Homes in Arkansas, which is more about building community than warehousing those in early recovery. 'Next Step' does not simply encourage the men in residence to form community, they must participate in house functions, work together on chores, stick together on outings and most importantly, they must participate in a vibrant church community. Faith-based programs aren't for everyone, but Jimmy has shown that when people are open to having such an experience, the church can provide an extremely strong framework on which people may build a new life and lifestyle. The men I have met from this program are generally returning from periods of incarceration. Their lives have been characterized by periods of indiscipline and unlawfulness followed by being locked in an unbending and harsh prison system. As they return to the world, they find they must assimilate quickly with few opportunities for missteps and the handicap of their "felon" status keeping them from advancement. Through the 'Next Step' system, they find safety in numbers, mentors, camaraderie and practical instruction on how to navigate the world on a day to day basis.

I recently had the privilege of witnessing the announcement that Next Step has partnered with a local church to build homes for people in recovery on donated acreage. In the announcement, the pastor discussed how they were building this community to 1) stop the housing discrimination of people that are felons and 2) create a community that maintains and preserves the values and structure that Next Step residents have learned during their time in the program. They are physically building a recovery town. This is a great example of the type of initiatives that are needed in our country. They are recognizing that the goal of recovery is a long-term process that stretches from today until forever. They also understand that when the individual struggles, it is the group that can pull them out. Next Step understands that the time in the house will be short so they are creating a way for men to live indefinitely in their positive structure.

My Original Tribe

Being Black or African-American in the US can be confusing, empowering, soul-crushing, sad, amazing, demoralizing and more. The list goes on forever. My journey as a Black man has been a twisted roller coaster due to my upbringing. I give my parents all the credit in the world for educating me in the way they did. For whatever reason, they believed that putting me in a predominantly white, somewhat exclusive, private school would be to my benefit and in truth, it has. I did gain the building blocks of a great education, and an understanding of how the world operates that many of my contemporaries do not share. The downside that I don't think they saw coming was the adoption of culture that excluded them. While I learned some really valuable skills and values, I also learned to see my own people and culture as "less than". I internalized self-hate and self-doubt. My internal monologue became a critic instead of a cheerleader. The residual effects still haunt me to this day.

My family was small and broken. As an only child, I had no siblings to reinforce any familial morals or creed. I was alone with my passions. This manifested in numerous ways, but I reference my first musical tastes. While my neighbors were listening to R&B and funk music, I was a diehard fan of the rock group KISS. While this isn't a fatal flaw, there were enough of these outlier tastes and interests that my mother made a decision to bring me back to the tribe. When I graduated from 8th grade, she chose to send me to another school, specifically to get me around more Black children.

My high school years were eye-opening for my identity and perceptions of the world. I had spent my younger years in a bubble of sorts. I often felt like an outsider but thought that my race was the cause. In high school, I discovered that my race had nothing to do with it. There, I met African-American kids that were at the top of the social hierarchy in scholarship, sports and social acumen. What's more, I met Black kids that had no need or desire to be accepted by white students. Our lunchroom was divided pretty clearly by race and though there was no outward tension or animosity, everyone knew to stay in their lane.

I left high school under a cloud. My addiction had started, though I was unaware, and I was caught selling drugs at school. I finished out the year at another school that was almost 100% African-American. I was completely out of place. From there, I went to college at an HBCU (Historically Black Colleges and Universities). For the first time, I think I felt "at home". I was at Xavier University of Louisiana in New Orleans and found New Orleans to be the most interesting place in the world, because of how they handled "racism". In Chicago, I had seen racism as an outward and direct act. I had been on buses when a black person said or did something out of order and the whole bus looked at any other black person with eyes that said, "Can't you do something about your person?" I had seen people beaten for being in the wrong neighborhood. I had heard angry mobs calling each other racial slurs. I had seen racism be an overt act. In New Orleans, it was 100% different for me. I found that the people of NOLA lived their racism as pretty much 2 separate societies. The white people just didn't see the black people and the black people didn't care.

I don't recall many instances of overt racism in New Orleans. What I learned there would be critical to the rest of my life. I learned that it wasn't just my "raised on the wrong side of the tracks" story that kept me apart from my community. Even in a place set up to support a person exactly like me, a school for black students in a city that wasn't actively trying to suppress me, I felt alone.

Today I am proud of my blackness. Life (and my choices) have led me to live in a predominately white, rural, midwestern town. My wife is white, and my children are mixed. I am aware of several situations where I am treated negatively or positively because of my race. I admit to using my blackness to my benefit sometimes. When all is said and done, I wouldn't change this part of my life experience. This is how my presently well-adjusted mind sees the world. The addicted part of me still looks to find validation for the premise that I was shortchanged from the start.

What is a Recovery Community?

My proposal is that we become intentional in building recovery communities. We live in the days of "The Great Opioid Settlement". With dollar amounts so staggering, it's beyond imagination, every organization with even remote ties to substance use disorders seems to be jockeying for funding. We have long known how the agencies, organizations, treatment providers and courts all work diligently to solve the problem but do so in silos. These entities will readily admit to being part of a larger system; however, their business strategies are often isolationist. Not one single day passes without someone reaching out with a new idea on how to spend "Opioid" money. The problem is no one knows how to free up this money. It has been swallowed by the bureaucracy and instead of a tidal wave of assistance and reform, we get sprinkles of funding for small unattached projects like the Chinese Water Torture funding method can eliminate the drug crisis.

There is an old adage that people are the average of the 5 people closest to them. Stated another way, if you hang out with 5 millionaires, you will be the 6th and if you hang out with 5 people that are broke, you will be the 6th. Anybody that has been vaguely around recovery has probably heard someone say "if you hang around a barbershop, you will eventually get a haircut." These sayings are how we share our common experience with contagion of bad behavior. They are vast simplifications but the message is clear. People are impacted both negatively and positively by those with whom they associate. If you hang around people that are in recovery, you will probably embrace those values and follow their lead.

The community solution may seem completely ridiculous to many in the industry, because it does what everyone claims, but doesn't seem willing to do. It really might solve the problem and put everyone on the clinical and support side out of work. The idea is to build the framework for the recovery community then have the various silos direct and compel their clients into it. I sometimes hear the protest that people should be allowed to choose if they want to participate. Why? They're dying! Some slow, some fast, but nonetheless, dying. Do we ask if someone wants to breathe? No, if they're choking, you free up the airway.

The other major problem from an "industry" viewpoint is the lack of control and revenue. If there was a strong and supportive recovery community, then treatment centers and clinical outfits would not have the ability to steer the proverbial ship. Almost every treatment center I know is very proud of their Alumni Program. Why do they have an Alumni Program? They would say they offer these programs to keep patients engaged in the recovery process. I say they are trying to trap the patient and make them dependent, just like the drugs they have just given up. Wouldn't it make more sense for the treatment centers to connect people with a vibrant recovery community in their home areas? The problem with that model is that the funds stop. No insurer is going to pay the center when the patient is finding their support free of charge in a network of peers and allies.

Recovery Communities are diverse systems and can have many forms. They can also have many rooms like a palace on a beautiful estate. A city may even have several recovery communities at the same time. We are not talking about how many meetings exist or the number of sober living homes. A recovery community is flourishing when all the various components are working together to create a momentum for the individual. Each stage of their recovery journey should be another step towards the center of the recovery community. I like using the term "cascading services", meaning the person is moving via referral to each successive and supportive service provider or support offering. This happens when treatment centers work with local meetings to introduce their patients.

The treatment centers don't just drop off a van full of guys at the meeting door, they actually make an effort to properly introduce their clients to the meeting members. The first step is for the treatment centers to explain the meetings properly or invite a representative from the meeting to explain the protocols of the room. This way, the patients are more likely to have a positive experience and want to return once they leave the facility. Meeting houses have to realize that recovery has to be all encompassing for newcomers. It is one thing for a guy with 20 years to only think about his recovery at his 1 hour meeting each week. A newcomer needs more meetings and more fellowship in between. Meeting houses have to become recovery centers that welcome people almost 24 hours a day. In this ROC (Recovery Oriented Community), there is a general value system that supports recovery and rewards for gains toward it. Likewise, as people distance themselves from the community, they begin to see the benefits of membership disappear. As we know, people in recovery respond to value add and value loss; logic suggests they will move toward the community as they grow and see value.

Let's be honest, this isn't a revolutionary idea. People have been trying to build "something to do now that I'm sober" for a while, but why are they often so lame and tired? I was a "downtown, skip the line at the hottest-place-in-town, nightclub drinker and drug addict." I like flash and glamour, I like excitement and if I am to be honest, a bit of chaos is always in style. Yet my local Alano club offers me a Sober Dance in the church basement that ends at 10:30 pm, serves Hawaiian Punch and has a guy who is

50 years sober (he was 20 when he came into the Program) as the DJ playing undanceable classic rock. Why would that be appealing to me? Better yet, how is that not making the recovery community into exactly what my mind tells me I don't want? I am afraid that sober life is going to be boring and dull. This dance only reinforces this thought. My wife is not an alcoholic. Would she want to go to this event with me? How do I invite my non-addicted friends and colleagues to such an event?

Our mission is to find a way to create events that take the place of our past activities without pointing a spotlight at the absence of our drugs of choice and lifestyle. That dance I described wasn't fun. It didn't relieve the longing I had for socialization with adults. It made me more bitter. It reinforced the idea that I was missing out on the "real" world. It said to me, "It's true, drinking does make things better". I needed the opposite. I needed a party that was so amazingly over-the-top that it blew my mind. I needed to be shown that this new life is full, beautiful and desirable. Otherwise, what's the point? As I have mentioned, I live on a recreational river. As I watch the neighbor's speedboats pull their laughing and joyous children on tubes back and forth, I long to be included. I know they are probably drinking responsibly, but as a newcomer, I would have to stand down on the "What If?" I have turn down the invitation because I cannot allow myself to get trapped in a situation that might lead me back to my addiction. I wanted to ride the river on the high-powered speedboat with the ladies in bikinis. Instead, I was offered a ride on an old-time unpowered raft and told to 'like it'.

One of my employees discussed a family with whom he is working. The son is almost 50 years old and has a severe case of alcoholism. This guy would drink until he literally could not walk and was eventually hospitalized. Our organization has been called to the Emergency Room at least a half dozen times to speak with him about options for treatment and entering recovery. His parents are enablers but complain about the situation incessantly. They call my employee at all hours, ask him to intervene with their son, to visit their home to discuss him and his condition. This family is as dysfunctional as they come, but the parents will not attend my employee's Family Group. They are clearly aware that there is a problem in their family, but they fear people finding out that they are seeking help. My employee confided that the parents have known him for years and have long sought his assistance even before he worked with my organization. These people know him in a very real way and yet, when they see him out and about town, they won't speak to him. He said he believes they don't want to be publicly associated with the guy that helps the "drunks". So here is the true impact of stigma. These people won't get help because of how it might look. As a result, they continue to enable their very sick son. Their support allows him to continue to drink in excess and eventually, he will succumb to the disease. At that point, they will claim he died of something else and move on. Unfortunately, no one at all will benefit from this situation. Not even the community at large, because this entire matter lives in the shadows of what is not discussed. This story takes a difficult turn. In the short time that it took to write this book, this man, the enabled son, left the structured environment of a sober, living home, relapsed in less than two weeks and was found two months later deceased due to drinking.

The ROC (Recovery Oriented Community) concept suggests that the stakeholders in our community have a duty to lift the stigma. The idea that people are judging you for asking for help has to be broken and replaced with a message telling people that they are only judged when they fail to see their situation honestly. In my entire life, I have never been part of a conversation about how pathetic anyone was because they asked for assistance. I know that my insecurities and fears want me to think people do that, but I have never seen it. It's a fiction that our diseases use to trick us into staying sick. In my life, I have seen that society moves on slogans. Remember "Just Say No?" What about a national slogan? - "It's OK, We Already Know. Just Do Something About It." I know, it's too long but you get the point. I guarantee the neighbors, the employers, family friends and acquaintances were aware and discussing the son that I described previously. If the parents' goal is to prop up their image, they're too late. Every nurse at the local hospital, every police officer that has done a "Wellness Check", every electric company employee that shut off the power to his apartment, knew that their son had a drinking problem. The most dangerous part of this is that most people will not let you know they are talking ill of you. That allows us to walk around oblivious to the cloud following our name. However, people will approach you and offer support and congratulations. They will remark that they saw your son and he looks great. To the ego-maniac, this doesn't seem like a good thing. They hear people saying they are less than. The stigma we find actually resides within them. They are full of self-hate and shame.

Community grows on familiarity and commonality. Think of all the ways we show social connection and availability. From bumper stickers to tattoos, yard signs and t-shirts, even our general fashion style is meant to tell the world which tribe you claim. The all-black goth look serves the same costuming goal as a lawyer's expensive suit. The clothing tells the world who the wearers sees themselves as and how to approach them. So even when a person wants to create distance from the world, they are giving off social indicators in relation to community. Have you ever wondered how couples with extreme perversions find one another or for that matter, people with intense criminal mindsets? We know that no one sits on a first date and declares that they like to eat tabby cats that they purchase at the mall. Yet somehow, people with the same interests and quirks can read each other from across the room.

Think about this - as a drug user, I could walk into any situation and find other users. Whether it was a classroom or a huge music festival. My mind is constantly scanning for familiarity. That guy is wearing the same shoe brand as me, her t-shirt has a band I like, this other guy mentioned a TV show that I watch... it goes on forever, a thousand times each second. My mind is always looking for a "safe port in the storm". How do I find safety in the world when safety comes from numbers?

I once attended a concert in a music venue that was round. I had the good fortune to have a seat on a second-floor balcony that allowed me to see the entire audience. Looking across about 1000 people, I found there was one woman that almost seemed to have a glow around her like in video games. She was "my type". She had the look I like but many women have that. There was something about her and the way she carried herself or presented to the world that said we would be compatible. I'll admit, I did nothing. I was shy. I just stayed with my friends and enjoyed the concert. After the show, we followed the crowd to a bar across the street. It turns out I matched her "list" as well. The young lady approached me and struck up a conversation. We ended up dating for a few months and really enjoyed one another's company.

People in recovery signal the world just like everyone else. Unfortunately, the growth of the ROC is hindered by a general misunderstanding of the concept of anonymity in the 12 step world. The idea of staying in the shadows made much more sense in the 1930s and 40s. That was a time when people kept a lot of the personal details to themselves. In 1935, the year Alcoholics Anonymous was founded, not only did you keep your alcoholism to yourself, you kept your sexuality, your race (if you could), your financial state, your political ideas and great business ideas to yourself. 1935 was not a time known for open-minded acceptance, not in the USA at least. It was during this period that jazz musicians were leaving the States because the combination of drug use and blackness painted a target on their back. It wouldn't be too long before J. Edgar Hoover and Joe McCarthy would each sow suspicion among citizens and literally impact US culture forever, but there is a wrinkle... Most definitions of recovery paraphrase "return to normal". If the goal of recovery is to assimilate with the mainstream and we consider "normal" as not having distinguishing characteristics, then our implied goal is to blend into the background. This makes sense because when considering the fact that the tail end of most addictions is anything but subtle, a return to not being the center of attention would be welcomed. In my case, I think I gauged a part of my recovery by how the Thanksgiving table chatter about my exploits and missteps had diminished. When it had shifted completely off of me as subject and turned to gossip about a cousin or an aunt's money or relationship problems, I knew I had arrived.

I've now given you way too many words, trying to express a very simple idea. **It's hard for people in recovery to find each other because recovery itself feels like a social camouflage.** If you are truly successful at it, no one knows. The camera pans across the thousands of people in the football stadium and we know that statistically, a great percentage of them are recovering from something, whether drugs, alcohol, porn, relationships... the "what" doesn't matter. What is significant is what could happen if all of those people could be aware of each other's struggles and be compassionate to each other's needs. As an afterthought, how many alcoholics in recovery have decided to enjoy a Cubs game and found themselves passing ice cold beers down the row from the vendor in the aisle? Could that be triggering? Is there no other way to handle this? Could there be a "sober" section?

Now that we've agreed that recovery is a little like Fight Club in that "we don't speak about fight club" way, let's really break some of the sacred cows. Undoubtedly, anyone who has participated in 12 step recovery has been told at some point, either don't make any major decisions in your life or don't date in the first year of sobriety. I call bullshit. I've always said that I don't think that this makes sense. My question to people is, if I'm in an abusive relationship or I get the opportunity to move to take the job I've been wanting my entire life, should I not pursue those things because I'm in the first year of sobriety? Of course not, that's the reason I got into recovery! Why would I delay the fruit of the most difficult thing I've ever done because someone arbitrarily thinks possibly <u>they</u> couldn't handle it at a year of sobriety? It doesn't necessarily speak to your own capabilities. I said the same thing about relationships. Again, I fall back on the idea that successful recovery is connecting with people. Where better to learn how to connect with people than in an environment where both myself and the person I'm dating have support, have a code of ethics and have a realistic chance to learn how to act with someone romantically in a healthier manner? Please understand the people I dated prior to getting into recovery half the time were high or drunk and the other half of the time, were people I was victimizing to take advantage of their money or resources. The people in the program at least know that they're dealing with somebody with these deceptive character traits. I remember when people would tell me in my first year that I shouldn't be looking to date anyone. My response was, "if Halle Berry calls and says she's willing to go out with me, I don't care how much sobriety time I have, I'm going." Of course that is an absurd idea, but the joke doesn't diminish the truth. There is no chance at all that I will pass on things I have longed for my entire life because the timing is off with my recovery. Instead, I see people reach for the Golden Ring and leave recovery behind, thinking they've found their source of happiness. I suggest the recovery community should rally around these people and support them as they reach for their goals, or date fabulously amazing movie stars. (It could happen...) In regard to this matter, the question was asked, "Is this fair to the movie star? Are they getting the best version of you if you are new to recovery?" My answer is that I don't know. There are no guarantees in life and I know plenty of people that don't have substance issues and cannot sustain a true relationship. The point of de-stigmatization is that my past addiction should not limit my present opportunities arbitrarily.

The real problem with a newcomer dating isn't the emotional issues that might develop. Alcoholics and addicts lying to one another and cheating on each other is somewhat inevitable. Moreover, it seems every meeting room I have ever been to, has a couple that met at the tables and has been married for a thousand years. So we know it can work. No, the problem is not that someone may get their feelings hurt. The problem is that someone may get their feelings hurt and stop coming to the meetings. In a town where there is only 1 meeting a week, you are really risking it when you get involved with anything that might become a wedge between you and the program in the future. When you are in a town like I was, Rockford, IL, there were plenty of other meetings to attend. It wasn't just the women I dated that I sometimes needed to give distance. There were men that I just didn't like or that didn't like me. Let's be honest, there were Exes of the women I was seeing... It could have been more a professional issue. though. Perhaps I was a teacher and needed to leave a meeting because a student was attending or an attorney on the wrong end of a divorce case and saw my client's ex-wife at a group. There has to be a larger sample size.

It seems every profession, hobby and interest has a "network". You ever notice how famous people seem to date and marry famous people and stockbrokers know each other. There are only 450 professional basketball players in the NBA during any given season. Considering the amount of people worldwide that play basketball, how can it be that the NBA players all know one another? It's because similar minds and situations seek one another out. As people at the amateur leagues notice their kids are really motivated for the sport, they put them in situations to play one another. Those kids meet and keep notice of one another as they age. As they enter each new level, the pool of people constricts, and it becomes easier to stay aware of colleagues. By the time they get to the elite levels of college play, they are familiar with one another and know many of the same coaches, programs and players.

We see the same network patterns in recovery. As people find themselves in long-term recovery, particularly when they are working in an activist role, they tend to move in small and intertwined circles. There are genuine "rockstars" in recovery. A man named Jimmy Hodges out of Chicago comes to mind. He was a regular at a near Northside club called the Mustard Seed. Jimmy was known to have a way with words and really speak in a way that caught the attention of newcomers. As I have traveled the country and heard conversations about AA in Chicago come up, not a small amount of those conversations turn to the question, "Have you heard Jimmy Hodges speak?" This is just one example. I find that every town has a guy that is well-known in this way. Social media is now adding a new level to this matter. I recently scrolled through recovery podcast listings on Spotify and found over 150 titles. People are saturating the internet with recovery messages. By doing so, they are breaking the stigma and normalizing recovery. With the influx of social media recovery, on-line meetings and many more paths to recovery, it is incredibly easy for people to connect with the idea of recovery, but these electronic connections will never replace real life interpersonal bonds based on a common goal.

Isolated 20 Feet from the Crowd

Loneliness was the discussion topic at my home group meeting today. The group is made up of people with sobriety periods ranging from 6 months to 50 years sober. Through the discussion, I realized that loneliness is a universal feeling. Where I thought I was unique in feeling like an outsider, I was simply experiencing a pillar of the human condition. We are individuals and though we constantly seek connection to others, we are in fact, alone. The difference or distinction of my case as a person with adjustment issues was the fact that I couldn't see that anyone else had this in common with me. I thought I was unique and was ill-equipped to deal with emotions. I used substances to numb the feelings but the chaos that this behavior caused only served to distance me from my fellows. I became a self-fulfilling prophecy of isolation.

In his 2020 book entitled *Together: The Healing Power of Human Connection in a Sometimes Lonely World*, former US Surgeon General Vivek H. Murthy, MD defines loneliness as "the subjective feeling that you're lacking the social connections you need. It can feel like being stranded, abandoned or cut off from the people with whom you belong - even if you're surrounded by other people. What's missing when you're lonely is the feeling of closeness, trust and the affection of genuine friends, loved ones and community." (pg8) Murthy goes on to describe people experiencing loneliness as not being impacted like an affliction, similar to a rash or wound. He says that it is a state of mind similar to depression. Loneliness creeps into one's life and holds a person in their most vulnerable state. The key to relieving loneliness, connecting with people, is exactly what the person is most unable to do. The only way to conquer loneliness is to shock the system and force oneself into association with people.

Murthy's book goes on to explore the importance of community in a variety of situations from illnesses to social media groups. In every case, he found that humans function better as a part of a network of supportive and responsive community members. Our concept of affinity groups in recovery serve to be an incubator for Dr. Murthy's prescription for recovery.

I have experienced recovery in many ways. There are times when I am almost ecstatic with gratitude for the fact that I've been able to turn my demons around. Those times are often countered by lengthy stretches of melancholy and hyper-emotional moodiness. Most recently, I have gone through a very cynical stage feeling that I don't have very many friends, and the people around me cannot or should not be trusted. This is recovery or, I should clarify, it is my recovery. Please keep in mind that my original problem was an emotional one, whereby I could not decipher the human condition in a way that allows me to meet adversity or uncertainty without the aid of a numbing substance. Today I don't have that substance. It is not an option. I still don't understand the world. I still get confused by people. I still get my feelings hurt, but now I have to deal with it without my protective shield.

As an alcoholic who used to drink alone and use drugs alone, there is still a part of me that retreats to my burrow when I am struggling. That part creates walls and pushes people out until my ego can bear to be seen as imperfect. Unfortunately, the bridges that you burn in this way are not often repaired. After years of setting oneself aside, I look up and realize that I am profoundly alone, even in a crowd of people. Even without my drug of choice, my "ism" can control me and separate me from the pack, where it is easier to hunt me. In those times when I'm feeling the lowest, I instinctively look for something or someone to attach a tether, for fear I might drift off into a sea of despair without any way back. Invariably, this is a connection with a person. I have to find someone in whom I can confide, find good counsel and take my attention off of my own problems. Earlier, I spoke of my "ism". I used the term as in alcoholism. In this case, I've heard around the tables that "ISM" can stand for "I See Me." As in, the world that is topsy-turvy, it's confusing. Inflation is running rampant. People are not getting enough to eat, children's education is poor and generally, the world is headed in the exact wrong direction. Yet, though I see all the problems in the world, I mostly see "me" and how it all impacts me. It's a very selfish and self-centered way of viewing the world. Our friend, poet Joseph Green, in his poem entitled "Talk Ugly" writes, "Do not think your pain has sharper teeth than anyone else's". Often, the addictive mind becomes convinced that the world is simply trying to do them in, regardless of their complicity. A mind in this state generally cannot heal itself. It needs outside input from another person who can break through the defenses and speak truth, showing the individual that they are just a small cog in a giant machine no greater or no less than any other.

Every drug treatment I have experienced, residential or not, was accompanied by the refrain "Change your people, places and things". For me, that meant a move to a new neighborhood or suburb, a new phone with zero contacts and a cut off of all remaining associates. The job, friends and funds were long gone, so I didn't have to worry about that. Here I was, 29 days sober, released into the world with a few phone numbers of "safe" folks (people I met in this treatment that would often relapse before I could even reach out). I was the loneliest I've ever felt, because I wanted to do right, but everyone and everything was a threat.

After my first treatment, I moved into a studio apartment in an old building. My 4th floor window overlooked the garden seating of a bar called Ranalli's. Let me explain - summer in Chicago has no better social spot than an outdoor table at Ranalli's in Lincoln Park. We're talking about a place that you can sit from brunch until the wee hours of the morning and watch people parade by in swimwear and summer fashion on their way to the beach and/or high-end shopping just a couple blocks away. When I say this place was buzzing, let me elaborate; I am describing the place in 1988. They're still open and doing the same thing right now, 40 years later! If you've ever seen a movie set in Chicago where the overly attractive young couple meet at a patio bar, it was probably filmed at this place. This is what was outside my window. 40 feet below my hot struggle pad was the most festive party in the city, 7 days and nights a week and I wasn't invited. Treatment had taught me that if I even set foot inside this place, I would immediately order a beer and ask for whiskey with a crack chaser!

The truth is - I don't know what would have happened. Instead of trying to be part of it, I sat in my window feeling jealous and angry. I tried to convince myself that all the people I heard laughing were miserable. They just didn't know the joy I found (yeah, right...). I went to meeting after meeting, 3 or 4 a day, hoping to find someone to call friend. I lied and said I could play the piano so I could join a band. I just wanted someone to hang out with. That lasted 1 rehearsal… problem is, after they saw I had lied, my pride wouldn't let me go back to that meeting.

I spent that summer in a deep state of self-pity. That's the summer that I saw a ghost and he saved my life. I was at my wits' end. I was at the point many people reach in early recovery "if this is what it's like to be sober, I don't want it!" I couldn't find a job. I hadn't been on a date in almost a year - no date, no lovin'. I had no friends, no money and the ever-present roar of Ranalli's as my soundtrack. I was ready to say the magic words - "F*** it!" Then the phone rang. It was a friend from college in New Orleans. She was calling to let me know that my friend/roommate/party partner had died when he passed out and our old apartment burned to the ground. She didn't say, but I knew that it had probably been due to carelessness cooking coke. I couldn't believe it. This was another omen. Why get sober when the end is the same? That night, I seriously considered going out for drugs. As I lay there trying to muster the courage to walk out the door, I saw a shadow in the corner. It caught my attention and seemed to move towards and through me. As the shadow passed over me, I felt a sensation of tingly calm. I felt I heard him tell me that he was at peace and not to use his death to justify my use. If I was that concerned, why hadn't I called him? What if I tried to get better instead of following him to an early grave?

I had a couple years of sobriety under my belt that time. I moved out of that apartment as soon as I found a job. I enrolled in law school, worked and spent way too much time pursuing a career in music. Eventually, I developed a new tribe in music. No, I didn't play piano. I was a rapper. I never really hit it as a "record on the radio" guy, but eventually I did pretty well in radio and TV commercials.

I flunked out of law school, got fired from job after job and I faded out of the 12 step community. I tried to be the "sober" guy in my music posse, but there were several starts and stops. It was tough being in my twenties in a city like Chicago and trying to have a "dry" social life. I was living with a couple guys I had grown up with in a beautiful townhouse in a trendy neighborhood. Our place became the house to hang out at, as one roommate, a professional chef, would cook Sunday brunch each week, complete with our lady bait, mimosas. I realize now that even when I wasn't using drugs and alcohol, they were part of my toolkit. I stayed as close as possible without tipping in, because I didn't know how to make friends or date someone without them being a little loopy. Or maybe I was just accustomed to buying friendships ... However you see it, there was a standing party there and I wanted to be at the center.

As life goes, I eventually met a woman and left the "frat house ". She became my entire universe and I backed away from friends, all of whom saw the writing on the wall. We were absolutely not a good fit. I have a joke I always fall back on when people ask me why I moved to a small town. "Like all the bad decisions in my life, I followed a woman!" I would use this reply and laugh over and over. Truth isn't far from fiction in this case. Truth - I lose my mind for women and make horrible decisions, but there is another part. That part is the component of my personality that truly doesn't know what it means to be in a relationship. My parents never modeled it for me and I am an only child that doesn't really know how to share. Therapy has shown me that my relationships are more about how the world looks at me in association with this woman, than my feelings toward her. In a sense, she is jewelry or some other status symbol that I hope will make the world like me. So it's not that I make bad decisions because of the woman's influence. I make bad decisions in matters related to the woman because I am codependent and desperately afraid to lose the person that I feel gives me social value.

So the relationship I started had all the mess that my love life would be. She was younger than me, of a different race and came from the other side of town, might as well have been from another country. We really didn't have much in common, but I tried to dazzle her with bullshit and access to parties. I am hazy on the courtship, but sure I provided an all-you-can drink lifestyle and I know I spent every penny I had entertaining her. I was heavy into recording music so we spent a great deal of time in studios and nightclubs. We were rubbing elbows with some of the most famous people in music on a pretty regular basis. I can see why it was exciting and had the promise of an interesting future. But it wasn't all fun and games. My girlfriend's mother was diagnosed with an aggressive cancer that unfortunately took her way too quickly. I don't think my girlfriend handled that well. I know I didn't. I was the worst. My selfishness and lack of compassion had me focused not on supporting them, but how I was impacted.

We spent a great deal of time in a strange social situation. Neither of us really fit into the other's world so we created a midpoint. She would go hang out with her tribes and I would be with mine. We would meet back late at night after partying with our friends for careless intimacy. As careless lifestyles tend to do, we got pregnant.

My National Recovery Tribe

I'm heading into a recovery conference in Chicago and it strikes me that I'm not terribly excited to go to the event today. There's nothing wrong. I don't have anything against the idea or promoters or anything of that nature, but it's Saturday at 7 o'clock in the morning and I just kind of would rather be in bed. That being said, I'm going because this is where my national recovery tribe is going to be. My group of people are leaders, advocates and crusaders in the mission to raise recovery in all aspects for people all over the country. I started getting calls probably 3 or 4 days prior from people confirming, "Let's get together to have coffee there", "We'll eat lunch together", "Hey let's sit together," etc. You know, the content is not as important as the camaraderie and connection of being in the same place and experiencing the thing together that this tribe brings me. I attend quite a few events of this nature and generally, the presented info is the same. I don't expect groundbreaking announcements like the reveal of the new Apple products. What I look forward to in these situations are the brief conversations with people I am accustomed to only seeing in virtual spaces. I love having a seemingly pointless conversation with someone that does what I do in another state. It allows me to humanize the people that I network with, usually by faceless email. It's very similar to what I found at nightclubs in my wild days.

My recovery tribe is very different today than it was several years ago. In fact, it may actually be a couple of tribes. Perhaps my work tribe and my recovery tribe are starting to blend in together and will eventually show themselves to be the same. I am a member of a home group and those 20 or so people know me completely separate and divorced from my role as Executive Director, Author, National Speaker, Committee Member at multiple levels and such. Those people who I consider my Home Group recovery community, listen to me talk about how I personally keep from picking up the next drink. The other tribe that I had called my recovery tribe, but now see are actually my career tribe, see me executing what recovery allows me to do. Which is to participate in the zeitgeist in a leadership role, trying to set policy and influence how others are impacted.

So, as I roll towards this event, I look forward to meeting new people and asking them to help with projects I have and, in turn, I offer to help with projects of theirs; commiserating about the pain and struggles of managing an organization that is grant driven and has a vague goal such as to "help" people. I guess I really just want to be in the presence of those people. I want to tell them that I'm proud of them and that I respect what they're doing and I want them to tell me the same. I gotta admit, there's some ego in there. I don't know for sure that I'm driving two hours all the way to Chicago solely to have people puff up my ego, because I genuinely do care and want to be part of this world, but sometimes, I recognize that my motives are selfish. That's what my tribe can allow me to explore, the good and the bad of myself. The fact is, no one is 100% altruistic and no one is 100% selfish. People exist in a space somewhere in between and I find that out through the interactions with the people of my various tribes. I find out who I am as a result of seeing my reflection in the eyes of others. So I'm looking forward to spending this time. I'm looking forward to hearing their stories, supporting them, cheering, planning and being a part of the success of someone else in my tribe.

Our Work is to Build a Recovery Community

Here's a "for instance". Imagine you had cancer and were receiving weekly treatments at a clinic. Every Thursday at 2pm, you walk in and there sits a guy named Tiberius (My example, I can pick the name). After a few weeks, you and Tiberius start chatting and by month 6, you're talking about the football game last Sunday and the kids and stuff. Then your doctor gives you the good news. Next week is your last treatment. You're cured. What happens to you and Tiberius? You probably say something like, "Hope we don't see each other again", laugh and part ways. That's how it goes. Occasionally, you hear about the "Saint" of a soul that keeps in touch with their Tiberius and they become blood brothers or some nonsense. However, 9 out of 10 times for me, I never see the guy again. What connected us was bad and it's gone. We are no longer connected.

I have seen the same thing in both my personal recovery and professional recovery work. One of the main goals of my organization is to have our Recovery Coaches create a connection with the individuals they are assisting. This should be relatively simple, as we meet the peers when they are at their lowest and according to all logic, they should be looking for a "friend". Nevertheless, the dynamic isn't the same as the cancer treatment example with Tiberius. In that case, both people were sharing a similar struggle. In our case, the Recovery Coach has no struggle. They are more equivalent to a nurse than a fellow patient. Our biggest issue is maintaining the connection with the peers once the crisis is over. The usual pattern is for the person to have frequent contact with our team for a while, during which they stay relatively clean and have few chaotic episodes. Then they go dark and we don't hear from them. We hope for the best, but we know this usually means they have returned to using. In all fairness, I will say that not all return to using immediately. Many times, the distancing indicates that they have returned to some other behavior that will eventually lead to a relapse such as a toxic relationship or criminal activities.

As I have stated previously, I entered the world of recovery community building due to self-interest. I needed to find people of similar state and status to help me not feel alone. In doing so,

I realized that our peer support system was the beginning of a courtship. Anytime you attempt to create a relationship on purpose, there are several identifiable steps in the process. Obviously, there has to be an introduction, followed by a demonstration of value. The next step is then placed upon the target of the approach. They must show interest in some way. The dreaded "waiting to see if they call" period in dating and interviewing. Once that reciprocal interest has been established, you can move into relationship building by compounding positive experiences to build history and deepen the connection.

This road to connection happens every day in our offices. People come to us when they want to find a way to stop being governed by their addictions. Most have been told that there is some magic sauce in going to inpatient residential treatment. We explain that treatment is only 1 option to enter recovery. True recovery can be found in giving oneself over to a new mindset and social framework. As ambassadors, we offer them a welcome to the recovery community. We then must promptly demonstrate our value by aiding the individual in some way; whether that be taking them to treatment, connecting them with other resources or simply being kind to them. Next we look for the spark, the first indication to proceed further on their part. This can be the first incoming call they make after the crisis has passed or the first time they show up at a meeting on their own. It is some action that shows they are willing to take a step toward what has been offered. At that point, it becomes a race to build positive experiences more quickly than the pressure and pain can build (which is a very individual matter) so that the person can incorporate this new approach into their life.

We frequently see people in early stages of recovery enter a honeymoon period where they are overly enthusiastic and giddy in their new freedom. This "Pink Cloud" as the old timers refer to it can be a major trap. The person can experience so much carefree success that they forget what their stress feels like. In doing so, they lose sight of the fact that the enthusiasm is masking the inevitable. Eventually, there will be an unmet need, a disappointment or a failure that will snap the person back to the reality of their situation. In that moment, they will have a choice to make and it will either be a reaction made from their newfound state of mind or their previous "tried and true", albeit destructive coping strategies. It is this moment that can make all the difference...

So the statement I made earlier about self-interest comes into play. Our goal was to build a community of people that support our own recovery and give us positive connections. We need people that can make the right choices intuitively. This gives me comfort in knowing that I don't always have to be the lone guardian of my recovery safety. It is certainly not lost on me that I can also suffer setbacks in my mental resilience and recovery. I too, am a part of the community of recovery and need support. My goal at 17 years sober is the same as a person who is 17 days clean and sober. I have to surround myself with people that will help me stay out of my disease.

I have had many "sobers". I often tell my peers that stopping is easy, but staying stopped is hard. I see it like a car. If I find I am driving out of control, I have to hit the brakes and pull over. That's detox and treatment. We take this time to slow the addiction and pull over to the side of the road, but like my car, if I take my foot off the brake, it starts rolling again. I have to reach over and shift the car from Drive to Park. You can't get out of the car safely until you do this and you're not in "Recovery" until you put your chaos in Park.

Parking an addiction means doing the things required to stay stopped. It means giving over to a new way of living with zero conditions. To follow the metaphor, what if you put your car in Park but sometimes, unexpectedly and for no reason, it would slip back into gear and roll away. There are not many things in this world that everyone agrees on, but I think we all agree that we don't want cars to unpredictably slip out of gear and drive themselves away without warning. Can we all get on the same page that we don't want our disease to flare up without warning and lead us to destroy our lives? So we offer a practical solution...give yourself over to a new life. This new life will necessarily require support and community. Yet the newcomer often resists this construct adamantly for a variety of reasons. They are fearful of things they don't understand. Their disease continues to tell them that they don't have a disease. The chaos has become comfortable and familiar. If we accept that the people we are discussing are not drinking and drugging for fun and they're not people that just have a slight issue with substances then we're talking about people with major substance use and mental health problems. We're talking about situations where Mom can't take it anymore, friends have given up, "stop or you're gonna die!" levels of severity. For them, there is no easy way to do fix the problem. Many times we hear these people saying they will "just stop". They think they will simply decide not to indulge anymore. You don't get to that point in addiction without building a support system of sorts around you. It just happens that the system is supporting your destruction.

The negative community consists of all the friends that condone one's substance use. The enabling family members that protest and argue but still lend money. The drug dealers and other users. This social system may seem happenstance, but in fact, it is a highly curated collection of people. I say curated because there are requirements that other friendships will not have. Remember, the user in this scenario is doing something illegal and takes place in a violent and unpredictable world. They have to trust the people they associate with to at least try not to get them arrested or worse. So now the hard part begins. We have to start actually building a positive community. How are we going to get people that are known to live in the shadows and hide their identity from the mainstream to come out and live out loud in recovery for the world to see? I often use the analogy of raccoons. You can't just go outside and call raccoons at night and tell them to come and hang out on your driveway. They just won't do it, but if you leave your trash bin out in an area where raccoons happen to be and they can get a free meal, you will get a congregation every single night.

Why is this? It's because they find value in something there that they want. This is the key. People are not very different from those raccoons. They want something that is valuable to them in exchange for their attention, attendance and involvement. Oftentimes people discount the recovery movement by thinking that these people just have nothing better to do so, why wouldn't they attend whatever it is that I'm putting together, whether that thing is good or not? People in recovery are just like anybody else; they work hard for their money. They have limited time and they want something that is worthwhile. We've tried everything to get people to come to our recovery center. At one point, we gave away a meal every day for lunch and that was pretty good. We found that Free Lunch always attracts a crowd. It has since I was in college, but we have to ask what kind of crowd gets together? In our case, we got a crowd of people that couldn't afford food. It became a gathering spot for people from all the local shelters. There were a few people who were attending other groups in our building that would stop over for lunch, but mostly it just became a glorified food insecurity project. The point is, it has to be of value to the people you're looking to gather on their terms and appetites. If you want to get young people together, you need to do things differently than if you want to get the older generation. If you want to get people who are into excitement, risk taking and high contact sports, you need to create something very different from if you were trying to get subdued well-healed, grandmotherly types. Recovery and people in recovery are not a monolith.

The Power of the Group

We have discussed how the individual finds connection and value in being a member of a group due to our instinctual need for sense of belonging. Nevertheless, how does one benefit directly by association with a group in recovery? Anyone that has attended a major sporting event knows that simply being in a crowd and expressing support for a team doesn't create the same level of comradery and mutual support as a much looser association among recovering addicts and alcoholics in a church basement for a 12 step meeting. It is true that the attendees of the game share a common hero; it is true they have all paid a premium to attend; it is true they all want to absorb and contribute to general crowd energy and excitement. In many ways, 12 step support meetings can feel like one is coming into synch with the other attendees in the same way. However, they differ, in that the sporting event attendees have no expectation of personal benefit and no agency over the group. In the support groups we are discussing, there is an expectation that I, as a member of the group, am not just a faceless soul contributing to the general roar. As a member of a supportive tribe, I matter. I participate in a trade of my attention, care and engagement in exchange for the same from the other members. As with any such transaction, it is my hope that I receive as much or more than I contribute. We'll consider some of these benefits.

Humans have overridden our pain logic. The group serves as a reminder for us of the human condition. I offer an example - I once had a dog that liked car rides in the back window of my mother's car. One time, he was in the car wearing a collar and leash and tried to jump out when we parked. Somehow, the leash got caught on the door, causing it to slam shut on him around his midsection. The dog howled in pain and fought to get disentangled from the vehicle. For the rest of that dog's life, it wouldn't get into that car without a major push from me. The dog remembered the car that tried to "eat" him, as I can assume he perceived it. It was an instinctive survival tactic. The funny thing is, he would get in other cars. So why is it that a dog can get the message that a certain situation is a threat and maintain a wary distance, but people can't? It is because we are hardwired to forget pain. Again, if people were to viscerally keep their pain in mind, no woman would ever have a second baby and football players would quit completely after the first hard hit. Humans have learned to value the pleasure or utility of a situation over their instinct to avoid the temporary discomfort caused by it. This is where groupthink helps us to remember. As a member of a group, I get to see what happens to people that forget that cars eat them.

We might rationalize that we are more intelligent than the dog and thus we are overcoming fears and making personal sacrifices that are beyond animals. In fact, if we apply our concept directly to substance use, there are many examples in nature of animals purposely ingesting foods that deliver a level of intoxication. However, other than lab experiments, we don't see animals going into full addiction, whereby they deny their nature and instinct. There are certain behaviors that we attribute almost exclusively to humans: sexual activity strictly for pleasure, telling jokes for humor's sake and it appears, addictive acceptance of negative consequences in trade for temporary pleasure.

When we trust the group and are transparent with them, the other members can help us to see our situation through an objective lens. Usually the group does not share our idiosyncratic quirks and whims, fears and frustrations so they can help the individual to make better choices.

The group also gives the benefit of distraction. It should surprise no one that people struggling with substance use disorders are keenly focused on whatever issues may plague them specifically. The Big Book of AA attributes the main problem of the "ism" to "selfishness and self-centeredness". Around the rooms, you will sometimes hear the "ISM" as an anagram for "I See Me", as in "I look at all the people in the world and when I consider who is suffering the most, I See Me".

There is another direct benefit for the individual from the group in establishing shared values. Hard as I try, I cannot be a trend or fashion. I can make a move or statement, but it takes the plurality of others to create a common characteristic. The impact of this is huge, because I, the individual, break my taboos regularly. Anyone that has tried to quit smoking can attest to telling themselves "no more" and then breaking that self-agreement. It is much harder to break our agreements with others. I have lost count of the times I've heard someone say they had a hard time returning to a 12 step group after a slip because they didn't want to admit to the group their failure. They could face it personally, they could recognize all the destructive implications and process them. What they couldn't handle was the shame of letting the group down. This is evidence of an implied pact between the group and the individual with certain privileges and duties. Most notably, the duty to stay in recovery as defined by the group, be that to be completely abstinent or at some level of control.

Being in this kind of social network was vitally important to my personal recovery. Prior to my current stretch of sobriety, I was the sober guy in a world of drunkenness and drugs. My friends used drugs, sold drugs and anything in between. We prided ourselves on personifying the hip hop ethos of the street player. At one point, I actually worked in a record company for an extremely high-ranking street gang leader. It should go without saying that the general drift of behavior would lead to crime, violence and poor decisions. Conversely, when I re-engaged with recovery by moving to Rockford, I joined a completely opposite social scene. I would estimate that 95% of the people I knew were members of AA. We socialized together, went to church together, often lived as roommates and supported one another. The key to my recovery was the complete immersion into the principles of the program. Our conversations never strayed too far from the Big Book. We set our calendars by the cadence of our meetings. The most important factor was the fear of complete isolation and ostracization of anyone that left the program and returned to use.

It can't be stressed enough that the key to the positive impact of the group is the level of honesty in both directions. Please accept that for this writer, evasion and failure to share equate to dishonesty. If a person is struggling and they sit among a group quietly not letting anyone know, for whatever reason, then they are being dishonest. Addiction doesn't pass people over because they are shy. In fact, the whole premise is that anything that separates us from connection creates an incubator for our sickness.

So there is a hard rule, you have to speak up. If you can allow the group to actually see you, warts and all, you open yourself to someone telling the truth. And we all know the truth is exactly the remedy to my insanity.

Example - I'm finding it hard to accept where my life is today. I frequently come to the group with issues around my home life and relationship with my wife. One day after a meeting, a friend pulled me aside. He said that after listening to me I might want to consider whether I am romanticizing the past and comparing the mythical past to the real present. The key to this was when he showed me how he recognized it in me because he had been doing this himself. He pointed out that I am looking at the greener seeming grass because I am focused on the pleasure of the past.

My first reaction of course was to debate and contest him. As I reflected on it, I eventually understood and agreed. Due to the quirk of the human mind that forgets pain, I don't actually remember my exes clearly. As absence makes the heart grow fonder, so goes my recollections. Each time I call them to mind, my ex-partners get more beautiful and exciting. Unfortunately, I live in real-time with my present wife and family and I cannot sanitize my experiences. I have resentment over the daily disturbances I encounter like the garage door being left open overnight for the millionth time. While my family today has to live in a real world with real life physics like aging and financial stress, my memories are frozen in time and only display the most flattering views.

This new understanding of my situation that was pointed out by the group also serves the group. I now am much less likely to bring this issue to the group for discussion. This is not to say that I now hold my tongue, it is quite the opposite. I can now bring my issue posed as a new question. Instead of asking" why do I find myself so unhappy with my family?", my new question is "why am I longing for the freedom and excitement of my past?". That is a much more important question because it opens the door to me discussing my fear of my mortality and lack of satisfaction with where I have taken my life. It's not her, it's me.

Beyond my own recovery, this encounter helped me to be a better support for other members. It demonstrated to me how to effectively bring feedback to someone without embarrassing or criticizing them. That is a skill that reaches beyond this group and bears fruit across all my tribes.

My Old Friends Tribe

I grew up in a really interesting time and place. I was born in 1965, 3 years before the assassination of Dr. Martin Luther King. The Civil Rights Movement was in full swing and the Black Community was just finding their way out of dark, dark times (no pun intended). Chicago is also one of the most racially segregated cities in America and at that time, there was even segregation within races. Not only were there Italian, Mexican, White and Black neighborhoods, those separated again by economic lines. My parents were well educated and had done fairly well for themselves. My father was an Attorney and my mother was a tenured teacher. We had some economic advantages but our greatest asset was our network.

My parents raised me in community with black people that had found their way into affluence during an extremely difficult period. We associated with black doctors, business owners, lawyers and entertainers. There were several neighborhoods on the south side of Chicago where these people congregated. We lived in an area called Pill Hill (a hill where a lot of doctors had once lived). There was a neighborhood called the Jackson Park Highlands and Hyde Park, Lake Meadows and Beverly Hills. These are the neighborhoods that I found most of my childhood friendships in. The children of these neighborhoods were usually very well educated and had experiences that most black children in the 1970s would not. Though racism was abundant, most of our parents had the means to insulate us from its effects. We grew up in a sheltered and comfortable bubble that encouraged us to reach beyond the stereotypes.

Today I don't spend much time with my old friends. We get together every once and a while for a holiday or such. When I am around them, I immediately think back to our past conceit. We would be the ones to take over the world. We had no barriers or boundaries. We've lost some of the original crew. I'll bet that a few are surprised I'm still around. The ones that are here are growing old but you can still see the children we were. The specific topics have changed from buying bicycle parts to build an empire to now, bitcoin and real estate. Most of us aren't as girl-crazy and I don't hear stories of fistfights. But the general playful banter and ribbing, the comfort of being with someone that has known you from the time you were born and the sense that you are among family never subsides. These people feel like "home".

This tribe is one that I am very separated from geographically. Just as it was in my childhood, I live far away and don't get to attend many events. This is the tribe that I think that my sense of self is most attached. For some reason that I cannot explain, my ego really needs me to exceed the expectations of this tribe. If I let down my guard and am candid, I really want some of my old friends to see this book on the store shelf and be impressed. I recognize that this is probably a character flaw and the source of much anxiety but it is also an asset. The positive side is the fact that much of the good things I have done in my life are the result of me wanting to prove my worth to this tribe.

I Found Out What Didn't Work

I had now been to Jails and Institutions. I could feel Death waiting right around the corner for his turn. So I started trying things to beat my addiction. Of course I would try going to meetings but as you will learn later, I didn't understand what 12 step was about and I wasn't open to learning. I tried to "fake it 'til you make it". I tried getting into relationships with people that were "not into that stuff". I think I tried every way I could find to get "right" that didn't require me to do much internal examination.

I had a period where I tried finding recovery in religion. There have been several occasions in my life where I decided I would get a tune-up on my soul and I started attending church. I have always liked the sound and energy of gospel music but I was raised Catholic. The Church of my childhood was slow and required you to be quiet, and frankly, I didn't understand much of it. If it wasn't in Latin, it was still Greek to me. So I would start auditioning my friend's churches. Most of the time I enjoyed the music, the ceremony and even the fellowship, but I never fully gave myself over to the faith. I just wasn't ready to honestly open up to the people.

I have met a great many people that have found what they are looking for in the pews. I know there are some well-established faith-based recovery programs and I support them all. They just didn't work for me. I absolutely believe in God and know that my recovery is a miracle. I just have a natural friction with the rituals and dogma. My mind operates in a way that makes me question people and institutions. I have faith in God but no faith in the men that are trying to deliver him to me. I prefer to witness God in action directly when I see people find recovery. I would eventually find God in the 12 steps.

With religion out as an option, mostly my sobriety tactic was to just pretend I didn't have a problem. I actually got pretty good at just stubbornly refusing to drink or drug while continuing to do absolutely everything associated with it. I loved being part of the party house for our social scene. Every weekend I found some kind of party, be it a football game or jazz brunch or anything to make myself the center of attention. I just didn't drink. If I didn't drink, I didn't do cocaine. Until I did...

Inevitably somebody would offer me a bump or a hit off a joint or something and I would take it without thinking of the outcome. Or, I would get a bunch of money or a huge problem or any other excuse, but I would make a decision to go find relief in a bottle or pipe. This happened time and time again...

From the start of the recovery movement in the 1930s the assumption has been that if we get people together who share the alcohol problem they will help each other to work out of that problem. As it goes alcoholism and Alcoholics Anonymous have proven this point to be true to an extent. The problem is within the people who fail to attach to the group. Initial recovery rates in the early days of AA were extremely high, some estimate as high as 80% still sober one year after introduction. Today it is much less, 10% is probably more accurate.

So what changed? Well, it was the introduction process. In the 1930s: 1) you were generally brought to the program or to the group by a member who "sponsored" you and introduced you to people. Today most people are being recommended to attend by an outside entity such as a rehab center, probation officer, family member etc. In the early days you were walked into your first meeting by a friend who stood at your elbow, today most people enter alone. We hear stories of people saying they felt different, alone, isolated, upon entry. Of course they feel those things. No one wants to walk into a group of people that know one another and be told to just "blend in". 2) Because of stigma and other social settings of the time, people were only introduced to meetings by someone that had worked the process. A few years back I had the occasion to speak to 120+ counselors and clinicians at a behavioral health organization. I asked how many had instructed someone to attend AA meetings. Every hand in the room went up. I then asked how many had attended a 12 step meeting. Roughly a dozen admitted to attending. My following question; how can you send a patient to a group that you don't know? There are 100 types of meetings out there - Men's, Women's, LGBTQ, strict and casual...the list goes on forever. You can't just send someone and tell them to go "get well". 3) Back then, everyone realized that this was a process. Today, 28 day treatment centers have changed how people see the process. Today, people think treatment is similar to getting a car fixed. You go in for your appointment, the counselors break out their tools and when you leave, you're "fixed". That is a supremely distorted and simplistic view of a very complex issue. No one is fixed after 28 days. In fact, they have just begun to see the issue in color. That is the "Start", not the "Finish".

My Family Tribe

Family is an interesting concept for me. I am an only child of a divorced couple. I have no history of what a nuclear family is. To me, "family" is me, the dog and my depressed mother who was either sleeping or shopping. A pretty grim picture. I have found a way around my issues though. I have created my own family many times over. Not in that I have multiple wives and pods of children, I mean I have family that I selected.

In my culture (probably the same in others but how would I know?), close friends of the family are regarded as relatives. My next door neighbors as a child were "Aunt Evelyn and Uncle Richard", My mother's best friend's son that lived 2 blocks down the street was my "Cousin" Kip thus making his mother my "Aunt Barbara". This identification was more than just a cordiality. These people actually assumed a parental surrogate role in my life. They were the people that my mother trusted to care for me when she couldn't. They were the proverbial "Village" that raised the child. I have carried this over into my adult life. I have become a part of villages that support people and their children. As a child, my father's side of the family was a bit of a mystery. We saw them occasionally and never really bonded very much. My paternal grandfather was a pretty large character in my life but beyond him, there was not much connection. I adored my father's mother. I called her "Big Gran" because she was tall. My maternal grandmother, "Little Gran", was under 5 feet tall. Ollie Mae, my Big Gran, was a flamboyant social butterfly. I don't recall her as the nurturing type. She was the roll on the block in a brand new convertible Cadillac (with car phone in 1973), pick me and any other kids that were with me up and take us to the toy store on a spending spree. She owned a small restaurant on Chicago's south side and was friendly with some pretty notorious people. She loved me to death as I loved her. But love on that side of the family looked like money and gifts so that's what she offered. I picked that trait up. A very close friend recently told me that my "love language" is gifting and money. I agree. When I want to reward my staff at work, I give them gift cards. My friend has said that in that situation, she would prefer time off work.

Today my family tribe is really diverse. I categorize things in my mind in some peculiar ways. As for who is in my family, I consider - if i became aware of an extinction level event that was coming and could only save family, who would I save? That is a short list. I would save my current partner and our 4 children, my ex and her husband and their children (2 are mine and 2 are theirs) and a few assorted other loosely associated people related to me by blood or marriage. That is who I consider my "Family" but not my tribe. When i look at my tribe of family I include a few people I work with who are closer to me than most family members. I believe that in my doomsday scenario, I would make room for my teammates as well.

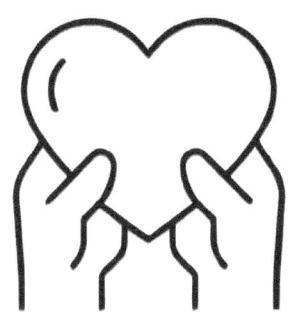

What You Won't Do for Love?

When people ask me why I moved to the small rural town of Dixon, IL., I often joke, "Like every bad decision in my life, I followed a woman". There is a little truth in every joke and in this one, it's my weakness for women. I can trace my absolute misunderstanding of women and the subsequent heartache and humiliation back to 6th grade. It's funny how the old hurts sometimes linger. I can picture the day almost like in a movie flashback. All the kids had started pairing off as "couples". Some of the longer relationships had lasted a week. Short ones were from recess until the end of the day. I think the only requisite to be a couple was, one of the two gathering the nerve to say, "Hey, you wanna be my girlfriend?" I didn't have the confidence to ask the popular girls. I was one of about 4 black kids in the class, so of course my peers thought I should look at the 2 black girls, Jennifer (my play cousin and best friend who I rode to school with every morning) or Marcia, a girl that had punched me and busted my lip a year earlier. (that's another ridiculous and embarrassing story) As for this couples thing, I did nothing. I pretended it didn't matter to me and waited. Eventually, one of the girls approached me and asked if I wanted to "date" her. She was cute, but not on the "A" list of our class. My self-esteem was so low that I thought people would value me by the status of the girl I paired with. Unfortunately that goofy idea still lingers in many ways. The funny thing is, in 6th grade, she was "meh". Today, she is an amazing woman that has gone on to do awesome things. Regardless, so we paired up. I finally had a girlfriend! Life was complete and I was part of the middle school zeitgeist. On day 3, she actually kissed me in the doorway of the auditorium. A week later, we hit the last day of the school year. As always, I would disappear into my other life until August. I guess I held some fantasy of long phone conversations and meetings at the movies with her over the summer. We'd been together for over a week, so it must be love... We got our yearbooks and began the ritual of getting signatures. I passed mine down the line and got to signing every book that came my way. I signed for Paul and Jim, Sandy and Mary, each with something I thought would be the most profound thing they ever read. We spent the entire morning passing books around. Sometime after lunch, I got mine back. I opened it to find all sorts of scribbles and nonsense. The only one I looked for was hers. What had she written? Page after page, I flipped all the way to the back of the book. There I found her note. Two words. "You'll do." I was devastated. Is there any way to interpret that message that doesn't take every one of my insecurities and dance them across my face? I was the minimum she would accept. 6th grade was tough, but here I am 50 years later, still feeling the sting of a "cute yearbook signature". Maybe because I felt the same. I was nothing special, extraordinary or valuable. I was "acceptable" when I wanted to be AMAZING. I hated that part of me and if I couldn't excel for the good, I wasn't going to let you see me try at all. If the best I could get was a satisfactory, a "C", from a 3rd tier girl with acne and braces, I must be a loser. It's funny how I spent a great deal of my life owning mediocrity and living up to it.

Today, I don't feel that way about myself. I still have insecurities, no doubt, but I see my recovery as a badge of honor and something of which I am extremely proud. Today, I recognize that I am a miracle and my social network has led me to see myself as far more capable and valuable than I previously thought. I wish I could say that I somehow found self-acceptance and worth by myself. The truth is completely the opposite. I found a community of people in recovery and through working in that community, helping people and connecting with them, I saw myself reflected in their eyes. I then learned to trust and accept that their view of me was more accurate than the self-diminishing, self-hating perception my mind and disease want me to embody.

8th Grade certainly wouldn't be the last (or even close to last) time I found myself confused and significantly damaged by my misunderstanding of women. My love life is a story of one mismatch after the next. I wish I could blame the women I encountered and say that I was "just trying to find love". The truth is, I never knew how to love unconditionally. I manipulated people, traded money and things for their affection, lied and generally did everything but love and accept them. To me, relationships were just one more way I could show the world my worth and I held women as emotional hostages to prove to everyone I could.

It wasn't until I came into a strong recovery community that I learned how to be honest about my intentions with a woman. We've all heard the phrase, "Don't date in your first year!" I add the exclamation point because that is usually how you hear it. I don't buy it. I say "Don't be a creepy, lying, needy bastard when dating in your first year" is what they should say. Let's face it. Women weren't throwing themselves at me in those last days of my using. Once I got clean and started coming back to life, I wanted female company. I was afraid to date woman that still drank and truthfully, I didn't really come into much contact with them. I was around women in the program and we were socializing. Guess what was going to happen…? But here is the difference. Before, my idea of a date was to take a woman to a bar or club where I was "somebody" and convince her to drink as much as I could afford. Then we would go back to one of our homes to let her do drugs until I got handsome. There really wasn't much more to it. It was expensive. It was easy, and it took zero emotional heavy lifting on my part. In recovery, I learned that I had to think about her well-being through all this. I couldn't take a woman out and get her drunk because our sober friends weren't going to stand for it. I also couldn't go "all in" and want to marry the woman after 3 dates because there was always a chance she would return to use and I couldn't go with her. Or what if I returned to using and took someone with me? Then, there was the shallow pool I was living in. In my wild Chicago times, I could meet a woman and run any kind of weird game I wanted because we probably would never see each other again after we split. I recall a woman that I dated for a short while named Michaela. She and I were pretty hot and heavy for a wild trip to Miami in an SUV filled with promotional vodka for a brand I was promoting. We had 2 weeks before the trip, a week in South Beach and a few days back in Chicago. Then she moved back to Czechoslovakia. A perfect relationship for someone like me at that time. I spent a considerable amount of time with her, but I am not sure that was her real name. It didn't matter. No sooner was she on the plane than I was out looking for my next conquest. My experiences in the recovery world wouldn't allow that any longer. My sponsor and my friends wouldn't allow that. They seemed ok with me tilting at the No First Year Rule, but they were absolutely not going to stand for me using the tables as a dating site and leaving a mess behind me. My sponsor told me that I could ask a woman out, but I had to tell her it was just fun and games. No running the "I'm looking for my forever mate" bullstuff. He said I had to be willing to bring her to a group event as my date and then never tell anyone what happened between us. That part is because he knew it wouldn't last and didn't want me messing up some woman's reputation. Mostly he said, don't be possessive and jealous because the woman was probably playing by the same rules.

I don't know that I've ever been the person that can walk up to a woman just say, "Hey, let's go on a date." I have friends who can walk into a room, and get the phone number of a woman solely for the purpose of gaining romantic company. For me, relationships of that sort are always partnerships. I look to build a common goal with someone I am interested in that way. There is a reason for the conversation; there is a purpose to continue the association; I doubt my own worth, I just know that. When I am looking back over the course of my life, most of my relationships have a 'let's build this' quality to them.

In college I had a friend that was a year ahead of me and I coveted his girlfriend with a purple passion. He graduated and went on to his next life step and I found myself in my Senior year with her being a sophomore. I don't think I waited until the second week of the semester to approach her and make a move. Shockingly (in hindsight), she seemed to like me and we "dated" for a few weeks. Then one night, we were out with some friends and she just started making out with another one of my friends. I was gut-punched. How could she do this to me? I was appalled. I was furious. Mostly, I was humiliated. I spent the rest of that semester in shame feeling that the entire school was laughing at me. How do I hide? I get and stay high. I spent my entire Senior year of college in a haze because of my reaction to this situation. It was not until I recovered and took a look at my part in things that I saw the truth(s). I was a shitty friend for hitting on my friend's ex (guy code). She was a shitty girlfriend to my friend. The friend that took her from me did exactly what I had done and would do in the same situation. I wasn't hiding because I was hurt by losing love. I hid because I wasn't trying to date her, I wanted to possess and control her. I was humiliated because I wanted to collect her like I had done with other women. In my mind, my value was linked to how you felt about the caliber of woman I was attached to at any given time. As I thought, she was the most beautiful girl in the school. My mindset - I should be attached to her and you should be impressed. We're talking all kinds of messed up here. The message though - as an alcoholic/addict, no matter what my part in this whole mess, I ended up sitting in a dorm room feeling sorry for myself and thinking I had been done wrong. This is where I could have used a few sets of objective eyes from the group. Someone to point out how I should have known the girl whose attention I stole would be ripe for another to do the same. Or that I shouldn't build my ego on my sexual conquests, as those ebb and flow like the tide.

Everybody's Looking for their Community and A Sense of Belonging

C hicago in 2025 is plagued with many of the issues that it saw back in the 70s and 80s when I was growing up. Most notably, the gang culture, and I admit that the gangs have become increasingly more violent in their behavior, but there was no lack of gang activity when I was young. I had the good fortune of having a father who was associated with the legal system, being a criminal defense lawyer and so he counseled me frequently about the limitations, dangers and problematic aspects of gang participation. That didn't stop me completely from behaving poorly and illegally, but at least it kept me in a mindset of trying to remain neutral in terms of gang affiliation. I was also scarred by an incident that happened when I was about 16.

My next-door neighbor, nicknamed Skipper, was much more involved in a lot of street-life activity. He was also my first and best friend. He and I spent many Christmas mornings playing with our toys together from the age of four or five. We spent hours sitting in our bedroom windows, which faced each other and talking on walkie-talkies. Generally, as we were both "only children", we found family in one another. His father was a police officer and he was a very kind man that I knew as "Uncle Richard". One night when I was about 19, I heard my dog barking and I went to the front window to find three or four young men messing with Skip's car. When they saw me look out the window and heard the dog barking, they took off walking up the block. I immediately called Skipper and told him that somebody had been outside messing with his car. He went out and looked at the car and to be honest, I'll never know what was wrong with the vehicle, but he and his father decided to go follow the young men. They got in their car and drove up the block, which was on a hill and I stood in the window watching as they went up the street into the darkness. Later that night, maybe an hour later, my mother got a call that Skipper's father had been killed. Apparently they had stopped the young men and as police often do, he made them stand along the wall so that he could search them. While he was searching one young man, another turned around, pulled a gun out and shot him. It was the most devastating thing I had experienced to that point. He died for nothing more than one group of kids who didn't like another group from the other side of a random busy street. I remember, I went to the scene and unfortunately, even hours later, I saw my friend's father, "Uncle Richard" laying dead on the sidewalk outside a liquor store at 93rd and Stony Island in Chicago. Even recalling the story brings me to tears.

That's what gangs meant to me. They meant stupid mischief that leads to death. They meant people killing one another over nothing at all and the interesting thing was, it was still poverty. I think I could've understood if I had met someone who was just fabulously rich and had done these things and changed their lives and made them into the King of Siam. Instead, what I saw were people that were just shades of poor killing each other over being a slight shade above or below. I wanted no part of it and I wanted out of that neighborhood as quickly as I could make it happen. And I lived in a good neighborhood. Today I recognize that gangs offer a sense of community just like we're talking about the recovery community. Young people from broken families, feeling left out, coming together to create an organization that gives them a sense of belonging, makes them feel protected, and believe that they have a chance. There's a book called Freakonomics that studies the structure of street gangs, and interestingly, It finds that most of the time they are networks that use people as expendable tools all to the benefit of a few that generally live outside the reach of the gang. I think the kids that are exploited understand that they are just pawns in the games of outsiders. I also think they allow that because of the benefit they get out of the arrangement. Most of the people I know from that world don't have terribly lofty goals. They certainly want to make a ton of money, but then the dream stops. I have rarely heard of someone wanting to make a fortune and move away. Generally, they want to get rich and then stay in the poor, broken neighborhood to wield power and influence.

Many years ago, I became transformed by a movie by Albert Brooks called 'Defending Your Life'. The central premise being that after death, we have to defend our life against our actions, and the main driver was fear. The movie suggested that people were afraid to live the life that the universe, or God wanted them to. I have come to understand that I was often driven by fear, but I don't believe that my life mission was to overcome fear. My life mission was to find the community that allowed me to move without fear. I often lived with a false, bravado promise of boldness. The Image of one who was ready to jump into the void. In truth, I am brave, bold and aggressive when I feel I am in the company of support.

I had been accepted to Howard University in my senior year of high school and was really excited about going there It pretty much had been the only option since I was a sophomore in high school. I had visited the school many times with friends. I had acquaintances that had gone there. Generally, that was the thought in my mind. But as I have mentioned prior, I got caught peddling drugs in school just a few weeks before graduation and I was expelled. Due to the fact that I had so deeply embarrassed my mother and was wearing a coat of shame myself, I jumped at the chance to get away. I say that as though I had a choice. My mother reached out to some connections and was able to get me accepted into a summer program at Xavier University in New Orleans. I got there at the beginning of my summer with the intent to stay for eight weeks for the summer program, return home and then go to Washington DC to attend Howard.

I got to Xavier and I realized a couple of things that were exciting to me. It was a small school that felt a lot like my high school. There were maybe 100 students in the yard for the summer program and I was able to quickly meet most of them. I was able to completely reinvent myself in this new environment. I was no longer the shamed, embarrassed, idiot. My best friend Jennifer was going there and a friend from the neighborhood Angie was going there. I met a young lady that seemed willing to date me. By the end of the six or eight weeks, I had made the decision to stay.

I really don't remember if I came home from the SOAR summer program or just stayed in New Orleans till the semester started. What I do remember is the first day of the semester. I bumped into a high school classmate of mine. Todd Lewis showed up. He was going to school there. Todd was one of those guys in high school I looked up to and I wanted his acceptance. I mentioned him earlier. Todd and I decided to room together in the dorm for a couple years and became incredibly good friends. He is still one of my dearest friends to this day.

As a child, one of the things that I remember about my father was interestingly, the presence of his fraternity paddle. I say, interestingly, because my father did not live with us, yet there were certain things that had been left behind in the divorce, one of which was his fraternity paddle. It was a foot and a half long, dark shiny wood paddle with the Greek letters, "Alpha Phi Alpha" engraved on it. It hung on the wall in the basement near the bar and oftentimes I would take it down and pretend it was some kind of a bat for baseball or cricket.

In the African-American community, fraternities were/are a badge of honor. Particularly at that time when the black middle class needed connection to one another. My mother was in a different organization. She was a member of Delta Sigma Theta. My father was never very active, but when we met other members of his organization, they all seemed to honor and revere him. My mother, on the other hand, was much more active and I could recall her having sorority meetings at the house where most of her close friends, women I had known from every aspect of life, from being my friend's, mothers to her coworkers would come over to the house. I never knew what they did at those meetings. I just know there was laughter, drinking and Mom making me clean up the house before they came. It just seemed like something you did once every few months.

One night in the first full weeks of the Fall semester at Xavier, me and my new roommate, also happened to be named Gerald, went to the girls' dormitory to pick up his girlfriend, a freshman named Jennifer I believe. When we got there, we were met by members of a fraternity called Omega Psi Phi. Omega were the cool guys on the yard, athletes and jocks. Apparently they had eyes on this young lady and wanted to tell two freshmen that we should probably get lost, because they were going to try to get her to join their auxiliary group or something. I don't remember exactly how it escalated, but I found myself instigating Gerald to fight these guys and as I recall, it turned into a shoving match, maybe even a fight and I was a part of it. I don't remember who won. I'm alive, so I guess I can only say that they didn't kill us, but I remember from that point on, wanting to distance myself from fraternities and trying in my mind to justify looking down on them. I think the truth was, I was afraid. I wanted to be a part of them, but I felt humiliated, fearful. Even later as my friends began to pledge, I would not allow myself to want to be a part of those organizations. I heard myself saying things like 'my father's in a fraternity and nobody in the fraternity does anything for him', 'so how can you say this will be good for my future?' I had friends that pledged all different fraternities, Alpha, Kappa, Omega, Sigma. Like I said, I justified my fear, my "otherness" as looking down on the frat guys needing to belong to something, and I was too cool. I didn't need it. It wasn't for me, But deep down inside, I wanted to do it. But I was just afraid So I went on with my life. In 1988 I graduated and returned home. I didn't think much about fraternities for the next 20 years. I eventually found myself in recovery and in Rockford, Illinois from 2008-2010 running a youth center. I was very aware of schools and what was going on with teens and education and things like that in the community. I saw an article about a local fraternity Phi Beta Sigma that was trying to get a charter school going. The president, who also happened to work for the school board, was a very charismatic person, Dr. Patrick Hardy. Dr. Hardy was trying to form a partnership with my youth center, so I reached out to him and I found out that he had attended Xavier University. However, it was many years after I had. We began to talk, and he asked me if I ever pledged. By that point, I wanted to be a part of something to give back. I wanted to be an upstanding citizen as opposed to wanting to be a rebel, so I committed, pledged and I became a member of the organization in 2010. Joining Phi Beta Sigma fraternity Inc. has been one of the true joys of my life. I sincerely say I wish I had done this earlier. I have found a great community in Sigma. I have been in several positions from the chapter level up to the regional board and my membership in this organization has become a part of my character and personality. As I look across, I see that it is associations of this nature that are the glue. We frequently will travel to events and most of the guys drink. Most drink responsibly. They all know that I don't drink, they all know what I do for a living. They all know that I'm in recovery and they accept me. They never force or even ask if I would like a drink, but I still go to the club, I still go to the gala, I still go to the cigar bar, I still go to the barbecue at their homes. I'm presently working with another organization to bring addiction awareness to the African-American fraternity and sorority world.

Conclusion

L et's get to that last hurdle, internal resistance. Please don't let my writing imply that it is easy to build a community of people in recovery. Remember, we are dealing with people that have known trauma, betrayal and disappointment and any number of other negative interactions with people. We have seen our greatest resistance to what we are trying to do, come from the very people we are aiming to assist. I heard someone say, "no one hates you more than the people you're trying to help". Believe me, this is not false.

There is an exclusionary concept in the 12 step traditions. It says that we are not going to see ourselves as professional 12 step practitioners. Generally, the average member of one of these communities asserts that anything you do to help someone else is sponsorship, and therefore peer support community building and other such activities are either Clinical, such as a counselor or CADC or they are being a professional sponsor. Nothing could be further from the truth. In fact, there's a very distinct difference between sponsorship and peer support. A true sponsor lacking ego, and the will to control another, will simply teach someone the principles and guidelines of the 12 step path that they are working i.e. the 12 steps. Peer support does just the opposite. Our goal is to try to bring people to the path of recovery so that someone can sponsor them while helping them to find employment, housing, and any other of a number of needs that they might express.

Reflections

I've recently taken a moment to look at some of the worst decisions I've made in my life since I started my recovery journey back when I was 18 years old. I was really interested to realize that most of my worst decisions , in fact, were made in periods of so-called sobriety. As you think about it, it makes sense. I was a heavy drug user. When I started using, I did not try to maintain my life or lifestyle. I would go 100 miles an hour, all in, no holds barred towards doom. I used every day all day and for the most part, it 100% consumed my attention. For me, a day of use started very early in the morning with me concocting some plan to get money and then repeating that plan throughout the day until whatever thread of an opportunity I saw had been exhausted.

Conversely, it was when I was in the sober moments that I made decisions on my occupation, relationships and other such issues with life impacting consequences. I was driving down the road recently, and I looked down at my hand and noticed a ring that I wear. It brought to mind a wedding ring I had from a wedding that should never have happened. In 1995 or 96, I was living in a sober home with a couple of guys and our "program" was to go to at least one meeting a week and as a crew, we would go to the nightclub to chase girls. Our rationale was that we were all together, so we would keep each other from drinking. Surprisingly, I stayed sober (dry) through this nonsense. Anyway, while at the club one night, I'm met a woman that I was attracted to, and she said she was attracted to me. I will not hide from the fact that I also was intrigued by the fact that she told me she was involved with a pretty famous member of the Chicago Bears football team at the time, but that she didn't want to be with him anymore; she wanted to be with me. There goes my ego. That played right into my "women as trophies" ideals. As things would have it, it didn't take very long for our dating to get pretty serious and somehow I was convinced that for one reason or another, it made sense for us to get married. I believe the case was that she had a daughter and in order for me to enroll the child in school or something, it made sense for us to be married. Whatever the reason, we're headed to Las Vegas for a quick marriage that my family thought was ridiculous, my friends thought was crazy and I thought made all the sense in the world. We couldn't go to Vegas to get married without rings and she had a friend who was a jeweler. For the bargain price $10,000, he would make us a great deal. Again, I was newly sober, love sprung and for the most part, generally pretty stupid, so I went to the bank and withdrew the $10,000, gave it to her and went to work or whatever I was doing at the time. She was to take care of the rings. Sure enough, a couple weeks later, she came back with two gorgeous rings. Hers had a giant diamond on it and mine was a gold band with five small diamonds inset. They were beautiful and I was proud. She told me that we knew that things for us from time to time would get tough, and we were always gonna stick together. As a commitment to that fact, neither of us could ever, for any reason, try to pawn our rings. I agreed. The fact that I referred to this marriage in the past tense should tell you it lasted all of about six months. We went to Las Vegas, got married, came back and argued. It was the craziest relationship I have ever experienced, full of her having some of the most dramatic and outrageous antics that I have ever seen in a person I've known. This includes her claiming that she had a neurological condition that caused her to freeze like an opossum when she got angry or scared and therefore, from time to time, she would just fall on the ground and lay there. I laugh because I recall one day getting into a squabble with her and she left the apartment in a huff. About 10 minutes later, my neighbor came and said "Hey, your wife is laying in the middle of the lawn". Anyway, six months later we separated, then divorced and went on our way.

You have to know where this is going; after a while, I decided having this ring sit in my jewelry box meant nothing and had no value. She had kept her ring. After seeing her at the divorce signing, I have never seen or heard from her again, so I decided to take my ring to a jewelry store and sell it. I was shocked to find out its value was less than $100. The diamonds were bogus. I don't know if her diamond was fake as well and she just kept the money or if she bought herself a really amazing diamond and shafted me. Whatever, these are the kind of decisions I would make because I alone give myself bad counsel and allow myself to act on emotion, even when I am clearly being taken advantage of.

I really can't say that being part of a recovery community would've saved me from a crazy marriage and wasting money. What I do know, is that the so-called recovery community I was in at the moment, meaning my two nightclubbing friends, were fully supportive of the relationship at the beginning. Of course, I did pull away from them once I found my lovely bride to be. I have to believe that had I been surrounded by clear thinking, sober and sane people, and sought to do things that would impress and be accepted by those people and I was being honest with them, I would not have gotten into that relationship.

Making crazy decisions of this nature did not stop there. I can name multiple horrible business decisions, friendships, real estate deals and any number of other thoughts that crossed my mind in the times between binges. I repeat, I am actually more dangerous when I am sober. When I'm using, I will retreat to my hovel, pull the shades and pretty much single mindedly consume my drug of choice without stopping for as long as possible. It is when I think my mind is clear, and I am allowing myself to utilize people, resources and opportunities that I can really create some interesting outcomes.

Whatever the case, regardless of the addiction, the struggle or the loneliness, this insatiable need to be in association with someone that I value and for that to be reciprocated, is the number one goal. It is a goal that usually is not met. The very premise being flawed, I find that no material object, grandiose achievement nor people pleasing gesture brings the connection needed to fill the void. Some in 12 step call this the God-shaped hole in our spirit that we try to fill with everything, but our faith.

I once looked for a definition of the word Spiritual. One of the definitions I found referred to being joined or related in spirit. They say that AA is a spiritual program, meaning we are connected by certain agreed upon concepts - steps, traditions, goals. When people speak of the "fellowship", this is what they mean. The collective of which self-proclaimed members identify as their extended and trusted support network. For me, it is what I've searched for my entire life, a group to which I belong that wants nothing more from me than for me to live well. When I have been blessed to find such connection, I have seen my life flourish and I have known happiness. It is not until I lose the connection that I again become victim to my demons. I challenge you, the reader, to consider this concept. Then I ask that you step out into the world looking for ways to create connection for yourself and others.

"We must all hang together, or assuredly we will all hang separately."

- Benjamin Franklin, 1776

www.ingramcontent.com/pod-product-compliance
Lightning Source LLC
Chambersburg PA
CBHW021107130626
46554CB00002B/577